I0234189

# A VOICE

FROM THE

# CONVICT CELL;

OR,

## LIFE AND CONVERSION

OF

# HENRY HOLLOWAY.

WITH AN ACCOUNT OF HIS TRIALS AND SUFFERINGS AS AN EVIL-
DOER: ALSO, THE BRIGHT SIDE OF HIS LIFE, AND SUCCESS
AS A PREACHER OF THE GOSPEL AMONG THE
WORKING CLASSES.

---

THIRD EDITION—FIFTEENTH THOUSAND.

## THIS EDITION CONTAINS MY MOTHER'S LAST WORDS.

---

MANCHESTER:
JOHN HEYWOOD, DEANSGATE.
LONDON: SIMPKIN, MARSHALL, & CO. AND" "OUR HAY AND MISSION
BOOK DEPOT, 33, MILE END ROAD.
GLASGOW: RELIGIOUS INSTITUTE BOOKS, 156, BUCHANAN
STREET, JOHN M'CALLUM & CO.

PRICE SIXPENCE; CLOTH, ONE SHILLING.

# A VOICE

FROM THE

# CONVICT CELL;

OR,

## LIFE AND CONVERSION

OF

# HENRY HOLLOWAY.

WITH AN ACCOUNT OF HIS TRIALS AND SUFFERINGS AS AN EVIL-
DOER: ALSO, THE BRIGHT SIDE OF HIS LIFE, AND SUCCESS
AS A PREACHER OF THE GOSPEL AMONG THE
WORKING CLASSES.

THIS EDITION CONTAINS MY MOTHER'S LAST WORDS.

MANCHESTER:
JOHN HEYWOOD, 141 AND 143, DEANSGATE
LONDON: SIMPKIN, MARSHALL, & Co.

# PREFACE.

City Orphan Home, Glasgow,
January 11th, 1877.

Three months ago Henry Holloway came to labour in connection with the Orphan Home Mission. From recommendations and reports which we had received of him we felt sure that he was well fitted to speak to the working and lower classes of our city; and from what has taken place at the meetings held every night, that conviction has been fully realised. From the simple statement of the Gospel and of what God had done for him many have been led to believe in Jesus, and are showing by their life the reality of the change which they have experienced. To God be all the praise. Mr. Holloway's book, "A Voice from the Convict Cell," or the dark and bright side of his life, is about to be reprinted for the third time; and from what we know of its usefulness to many in connection with our work we believe that it is well fitted to awaken the interest of the careless to the fact that God is willing and ready to save to the uttermost all who come to Him through Jesus. The book has had an influence on old and young, as the following cases will show: A little boy of 13 years, who had attended Sunday school from an early age, but did not know that he was a sinner till he read Mr. Holloway's book, by the Spirit of God was led to trust in the Saviour. Another case is that of an elderly man who had been brought up by pious parents, but had departed from the right way. He got Mr. Holloway's book, and was arrested and led to trust in the Lord. These are only samples from dozens of cases we know, and we very heartily recommend the book to the prayerful perusal of all.

WM. QUARRIER,
Founder of the City Orphan Home, Glasgow.

Dear Reader,—My motive for publishing the Third Edition of this book is to exalt Christ in the affection of His people, not to glory in wrong-doing. God forbid that I should glory save in the cross of our Lord Jesus Christ. I lay the book at His feet, saying, " Lord, Thou knowest the desire of my heart. Use these pages to Thy glory."

Yours truly,

HENRY HOLLOWAY.

# LIFE OF HENRY HOLLOWAY.

I was born in Birmingham on the 18th September, 1840. When only three years of age I had the misfortune to lose my father. He passed from time to eternity, leaving my mother to fight the battle of life with three young children—the eldest only seven years of age, the youngest sixteen months. Having in her heart the love of Christ, she looked with fervent trust to the strong for strength; and often did she take us to the footstool of the throne of grace to implore God to aid her in her struggles with sin and sorrow, and to be, in accordance with His loving promise, a husband to the widow and a father to the fatherless; remembering His gracious covenant with the righteous never to suffer them to be forsaken nor their seed to beg bread (Psalm xxxvii., 25).

That my mother had need of help was only too apparent; but her sense of the responsibility devolving upon her, and the feeling of self-reliance which had been implanted within her, caused her to struggle hopefully on; and, with the assistance of a mangle, she was enabled to support both herself and her children. Time rolled on, and my eldest brother having arrived at an age when he was deemed fit to go to work, he was bound apprentice to learn a trade. His master was very kind to him, and did what he could to push him on in acquiring a knowledge of his craft. He also rendered a little assistance to my mother. I was still attending school; and when only ten years of age I attracted attention by my knowledge of the Scriptures, and frequently obtained the first prize in the Sunday school for repeating Bible lessons.

Not long after this my mother married again with a man who had a family of children. All went on very well for a time, but at length a cloud settled on our homestead which threatened to entirely destroy its peace. My stepfather turned out to be a very drunken man; and it soon became only too obvious that his conduct was undermining my mother's health, and that if persisted in must eventually break her heart and bring her with sorrow to the grave. But in the midst of her grief and the troubles with which she had to contend she took great care of me, doing all she could to teach me the right way, and to keep me from falling away from obedience to God. Her husband was not long ere he took to ill-using her when in drink, in a way that did not at all agree with my feelings. Being of a somewhat lively disposition, not without spirit, and strongly attached to my mother, I could not calmly stand by and see her beaten. On one occasion I stepped between them, with the intention of giving him to understand that I should not allow his brutality to be continued without some attempt on my part, feeble though it might be, to check it. No doubt he regarded me at the moment with no small amount of contempt, for he seized me and threw me into the street, and swore that he would not permit me to remain in the house. On several occasions afterwards, in order to obtain admittance, I had to climb the cistern wall, and my mother helped me through the back window. One of his sons having one day become aware of my presence in the house, informed him of the fact. This so enraged him that he again fell foul of my mother, and gave her a couple of black eyes. This was really more than I, young as I was, could or ought to stand; for I felt that she was my mother—that I had her in my heart, and that I was in hers, for many a time have I found her on her knees weeping and praying that God would bless the lads, especially Harry. I had been taken in by a kindly neighbour, and sheltered several nights; but hearing of the way my mother had been maltreated I ran into the house, with a purpose merely half defined, but only to be again turned into the street.

Very shortly after this event I unfortunately became associated with evil company—with lads that had already got the seeds of sin sown in their hearts. I had no conception at the time that one false step might carry me into the path that leads to certain destruction. It was summer time, and I and my new companions used to go into the hayfields to sleep. Several of them persuaded me and another, then as guileless as myself, to go with them to steal fruit from a garden in Rusholme. Justice, however, soon overtook us. We were apprehended, and taken to the New Bailey Prison (two of the party being old offenders), I was afraid lest I should have to undergo a term of imprisonment; but just as Mr. Trafford, before whom we were tried, was about to commit me to gaol, my mother, who had heard of my apprehension, stepped into the witness-box, and, with tears in her eyes, pleaded for my liberation, and successfully, too, for I was discharged with a caution. My two companions in crime were each sentenced to seven days' imprisonment. This was my first violation of the principle of honesty, and the remembrance of it brings to my mind the truth of the following lines :—

> Oft you see the young beginner
> Practice little pilfering ways,
> Till, grown up an hardened sinner,
> Perhaps the gallows ends his days.

On leaving the court I went home with my mother, but not to stay, for my stepfather soon began again to beat her in my presence, and this I could not bear to see. So soon as my old associates, therefore, were released, I was in their company again. At this time I got a situation in a ropewalk, and being there mixed up with evil men and lads I soon acquired the habit of cursing and swearing as badly as any of them. Now and then, when things did not go right, the master belaboured me with a rope, and swore at me in a most vehement manner. This did not suit me at all, so at length, in company with the lad who turned the wheel, I ran away. When Saturday came, going home without our wages (3s. each) was more than we durst venture on, so we resolved to stay out together at nights, and sleep where we could. We often earned sixpence or a shilling in the markets, which, however, was spent in visiting the Casino or theatre. During all this time my mother had no idea where I was, nor how I was spending my time.

My associates had now become more numerous. I had formed a too close acquaintance with evil youths, some of whom had more than once been the inmates of a prison. I was now fourteen years of age. One day, whilst in company with these associates, I was taken to the station-house and charged with having committed a felony, of which I was entirely innocent; and as I shall have to answer before God for all I may say in this book, the reader must not doubt that in this declaration I speak the absolute truth. Next day I was taken to the court for examination. I had already made my mother acquainted with the affair. She was in court during the trial, but all she could say to obtain my release proved unavailing, I was sent to prison for two months, with hard labour. Whilst in prison I was so enraged at the idea of being unjustly incarcerated that I became unruly, and wanted my own way. For this I was severely punished, by being placed in dark cells and restricted in my food to bread and water.

Dear reader, I most solemnly and earnestly warn you here to shun wicked company. This was the first sentence pronounced against me, and, although years have passed away, I am none the less impressed with the fact that I suffered innocently. How true are the words, " He that is partner with a thief shall smart for it ; though hand join in hand the wicked shall not be unpunished." (Proverbs xi., 21.)

My term of imprisonment having expired I was liberated. My mother met me at the prison gates to take me home again, but the feeling aroused by the reflection that I had suffered wrongfully had become so rooted and intense that I could not become reconciled or contented. Shortly afterwards I was in company with a youth, and our conversation turning upon the punishment I had undergone, he said to me, "Harry, it was me and Tom that committed that robbery." The Tom here referred to was the lad who got two months along with me. I was so exasperated at this confession being so impudently made to my face, that I felt almost irresistibly inclined to throw the guilty youth into a large hole which some men were engaged in excavating for the foundation of a building; but a second thought obtained the mastery over me, and I allowed him to go his way unhurt.

By this time a spirit of recklessness had so taken possession of me that I began to care for nothing, but, above all, to lose sight of the precious counsel I had received from my mother; and I was not long before I was apprehended again. As, however, nothing could be proved against me, I was discharged  The youth charged along with me was found guilty, and sentenced to one month's imprisonment, with hard labour. I began now to reflect a little upon my position, and to feel afraid that if I persisted in the course of life in which I had become entangled justice would certainly overtake me. Better thoughts prevailed over those that had unfortunately incited me to action, and I resolved to forsake bad company, go to work, and do better. I was taken to work by an uncle, and was used very well in every way. One day, however, whilst going an errand, I again fell in with bad company, and was tempted to leave my work. I was soon afterwards again in the hands of the police, and for my offence was sentenced to three month's imprisonment, with hard labour. I did not think much about the matter until I got into my cell. Solitude then induced reflection, and I began to ask myself what would be the end of all this, more especially as I well knew right from wrong. My mother's counsel, the advice of friends, the teachings of the Sunday school, and all the precious influences of the past, crowded into my mind, and I could not restrain the tears which coursed down my cheeks. The words (Proverbs xiii., 15), "The way of transgressors is hard," came vividly before me. Well, thought I, I have made my bed for three months, anyway, and I shall have to lie upon it.

Whilst in prison this time I was put to learn mat-making for a portion of the time ; the rest of my term being passed at the crank, turning each day fourteen thousand revolutions. "The way of transgressors *is* hard." But this was not all the punishment I had to endure ; I was sent to the dark cells for talking in the exercise-yard.

On receiving my discharge my mother obtained for me a situation in a gentleman's house as page-boy. I was not so well clad at the time, but they gave me a new suit of clothes. The family liked me very much, and I liked them, too. There was one thing, however, that I did not relish, and that was being without money. Soon after I entered this service I formed an acquaintance with a young gentleman who lived close by, and who had plenty of money. Where he got it from I did not know, nor did I care, so that I was allowed to share it with him. His habit was to visit hotels and theatres, and he would always have me with him when I was at liberty to go out. My occupation consisted of cleaning boots, brushing clothes, and carrying messages to the warehouse in town, &c. When brushing my master's clothes I several times felt money in the pockets, and the question suggested itself, Does my master know of its being there? But I made a resolution never to be dishonest where I was employed and so resisted the temptation. This was one reason why I was liked.

As I grew older I began to take drink, and to keep higher company than formerly. As a consequence my duties became neglected, and although only seventeen years of age I was often taken from the public-house door in a state of inebriation. Dear reader, as a friend, and one who has been within its fatal grasp, if you are a partaker of intoxicating liquor, let me implore you to give up the habit. It was the primary cause of my wicked and most daring career. I have learned, by experience, that it is the fruitful parent of untold misery, the grave of all comfort, the destroyer of everything that is good and noble, and the manufacturer of nearly every kind of suffering; it is the fountain whence springs life's bitterest streams; the most blighting ingredient in the broken-hearted wife's domestic cup, and the severest pang that calls forth the children's wail; it is the fatal point of the murderer's dagger, the poison in which the devil dips his most barbed arrows, the piercing sting of the pauper's lot, and the most dismal clank of the prisoner's chains. The beerhouse is the infernal battery whose fatal shots are slaughtering humanity by thousands. It is daily digging premature graves for wrecked bodies, and kindling the sulphurous fires of hell for lost souls. This is strong language; but is it not true that no drunkard shall inherit the kingdom of heaven? And if we go not there we must assuredly go to hell. Take warning, then, my friends. I would not have written this book if it were not to do you good, and to prevail upon you to seek that Saviour who had mercy upon me. The beerhouse I can say, without hesitation, is the fool's college, where men and women graduate for every species of crime, and where they learn the horrid art of getting by the shortest road to hell. The liquor traffic is the devil's express train, whose crowded freight of maddened souls start from rum and brandy on the line of dissipation. The engine driver is folly; the boiler is heated with the fire of frenzied passions, and the engine is impelled by the steam of inebriated excitement. The thoughtless passengers are all booked for the entire journey, without return tickets; and they are all in a hurry to reach the terminus of their damnation. Drink makes wise men fools, rich men beg gars, and honourable men into something worse than brutes; it defaces beauty, enfeebles strength, empties the purse, ruins health, manufactures wholesale misery, and prostitutes the noblest instincts of man's better nature. It peoples the workhouse, is the pauper's pay-master, the prisoner's lash, the murderer's knife, the criminal's rope, the devil's recruiting sergeant, the nation's great funeral undertaker and coffin-maker, the world's curse, and, to come to myself, it led to my down-fall from the good situation I was now in. I got so addicted to it, so enslaved by it, that every penny I could get went to the alehouse. In a few days only after I was discharged from my situation I was, with another man, in the hands of the police again, charged with felony. On being brought before the court I was recommended to mercy on account of the good character given me by my last employer, and escaped with the minor punishment of two months' imprisonment, but supplemented with three dozen lashes. This time I was incarcerated in the New Bailey Prison, at Salford (now taken down). I shall never forget the morning I was brought out to be flogged, which happened about a week after I went in. When I got into the great yard I saw the governor, the surgeon, the chaplain, and about forty prisoners, the latter with their faces towards the wall. When the triangle was brought out I began to shake from head to foot. It appeared that several prisoners were to be flogged; and to make matters more unpleasant, so far as I was concerned, a number were to undergo the punishment before me. When the first was strapped he began to shout and roar like a child, but the lash was, nevertheless, administered with great force. Such crying out and groaning I never heard before or since, and I hope may never hear again. Amongst the rest were the following ejaculations: "Do have pity!" "Lord, save me!" "Mercy! mercy! you'll kill me!" My name was called at last, and I in turn began to cry for pardon and mercy; but it was only like the prophets of Baal calling unto their god—no help came. On the contrary, the more I cried for mercy the more severely was the lash felt. At length I was released from the triangle and marched slowly to my cell. On arriving there I fell down from exhaustion, and was scarcely able to lie in bed for pain. Whilst in this state I began to think that I was going on in a fair way for the hulks. The Spirit of God often strove with me, but made no lasting impression neither on my heart or mind. The day after I was flogged the warder came into my cell, and said, "They have been warming your back, have they?" So hardened was I that I asked him what it had to do with him. He said he would report me, but thought better of it. As I got better the thought of the lash grew weaker, and I began to care very little about anything else. When I got out of prison again I became worse than ever, and in less than four months I was put upon my trial again for felony, but was not convicted. On then I went in my mad career, not caring for anything. I picked up new associates—bad men like myself. Having lost sight of going to work again, nothing appeared to remain for me to do but to be a man of the world. I was now away from home, but my mother's prayer haunted me—"Bless the lads, but especially Harry."

In three short weeks after this I was apprehended on a charge of forgery, and sent for trial.

I was once more attired in prison dress, and it entered into my thoughts that now there was no hope for me, and that I should have to be transported. In addition to this was the racking reflection that I was bringing down the grey hairs of my mother with sorrow to the grave. Her prayers haunted me night and day, and often, when sitting alone in my dreary cell, did I wish that Death would lay his icy hand upon my heart ere my trial came on ; and, although leading the life that I was, I might often have been seen prostrate on my knees in that cell imploring God to save me from the galling curse that bound me——

that of dishonesty and drunkenness—the very curse that was mainly instrumental in making me what I was hereafter. I knew well that my mother would be beaten by my stepfather, and I was not mistaken. The very day that he heard of me being again in custody he called me some harsh name. "Well," replied my mother, "I cannot help it. He is my son, and let him do what he will, and let the consequences be what they may, he shall have a home in my heart if he cannot have one in the house." The following Tuesday my mother came to see me in prison, and no sooner did her eyes encounter mine than she burst into tears. Her heart was full to overflowing, "Don't weep, mother," I said; "it's a long lane that has never a turn." "Ah, my lad," was her response, "you have gone along this road long enough. Remember, 'the wages of sin is death.' I have never ceased to pray for you since you were taken; and if the Lord and the law will give you another chance I hope you will do better." I said, "I will, mother.'

All that was done in my own strength and soon forgotten. I went back to my cell with a heavy heart, and when there could not help weeping. I shall never forget how earnestly I cried to God, if it pleased Him, to stop me in my bad career. The language of my heart that day was this :—

> When on my bed of care I lie,
>   Locked in this dismal cell,
> Deprived of my dear mother's care,
>   And those I loved so well—
>
> Thou God of grace look down on them,
>   To them Thy mercy show—
> Dear Jesus, pity my distress :
>   My tears like fountains flow.
>
> Though my afflictions are severe,
>   Thy judgment is quite right ;
> For, Lord, ten thousand are my crimes,
>   And sinful in Thy sight.

When brought up for trial the first sight that met my eyes on entering the court was my mother, weeping; and on looking around I saw several persons whom I knew. The trial lasted a long time. At its close the jury found me guilty, but I was once more recommended to mercy. My mother also came forward and pleaded for me. The judge, however, said, " My dear woman, if you were to bring all Manchester to speak for him they could say no more than the last witness." This was a gentleman for whom I had worked. He not only gave me a good character, but said had I wanted the money, to gain which I had resorted to forgery, he would have lent it to me with pleasure; and if it should be that justice would deal leniently with me he would employ me again. The foreman of the jury rose again and begged that the judge would give me another chance of doing well. The judge then turned to me and, addressing me, said, " If it had not been for the character given to you by your last employer I should most assuredly have sent you into penal servitude. I shall give you another chance of doing right and recovering your fallen position. The sentence that I am about to pass on you is that you be sent to prison for three calendar months, with hard labour; hoping that you will do well when you come out." For a moment I was almost speechless. When I recovered the use of my tongue I faltered out, " Thank you, sir." I was removed from the dock quite light-hearted with the thought of having got off so well. When in my cell I could not help thinking, " Well, is not the Lord and the law good to me? If ever I go before the judge again he will warm me up; and serve me right."

Time rolled on; the three months expired, and I was once more free. I was met at the prison gate by an old companion in sin, and ere we had walked one hundred yards I was in the public-house with him and a few more of my old pals, and there got so drunk that I lost all consciousness of what I was doing. When I awoke I would seek the accursed drink yet again. Once more, like the Prodigal Son, I was in the house of sin—the house that leads to hell and the chamber of death; for, "at the windows of my house I looked through my casement, and, behold, among the simple ones I discerned a young man void of understanding." That was myself. I was led captive by the Devil at his will, and the heart that was soft and had been melted to tears was more branded than ever. The course of sin and crime I still pursued, declining to listen to advice from anyone. My own way I would have.

Soon afterwards I had to leave the town of Manchester, for reasons well known to the police and myself. I had a companion in my flight, to whom I said, " Cast in thy lot with me ; let us both have one purse." Ah ! but my sandglass had almost run down ! " Though hand join in hand the wicked shall not be unpunished ; his own iniquities shall overtake him, and in the greatness of his folly he shall go astray." And, oh, dear reader, it was so with me. I became worse than ever.

I shall abstain from furnishing the details of the several horrid and daring robberies in which I have been concerned ; for excellent reasons it is not desirable to place upon record the *modus operandi* of anyone. This book has, by God's blessing, been written to show those who may be in the wretched position I once was that they need not despair. The same God that saved me can save the vilest.

About this time I heard that my mother was anxiously searching for me, and one day, whilst I was playing cards in a public-house, she entered. As soon as she saw me, " Oh, Harry," she cried, " I have sought you sorrowing night and day," and she began to weep, and, in agony, cried out, " Do, my lad, come away from that card table ; it will ruin you." Although I still resisted advice I often had to smart for it. " The rod and reproof give wisdom, but the child left to himself bringeth his mother to shame."

It was not long after this ere I resolved to give my evil course up ; but my resolutions were always made in my own strength. How true is the word of God, where it saith, " Trust in the Lord with all thy strength, and lean not unto thine own understanding : in all thy ways acknowledge him, and he shall direct thy paths." But " the wicked is driven away in his wickedness." " The candle of the wicked shall be put out."

In pursuance of my resolve I went to work, and for a time did well. But the cursed drink I could not give up. I spent all I could get upon it, and often starved my body to appease my insatiate longings for it. Like the grave, my morbid appetite was ever crying, " Give, give, give !" I again, for drink, left my work. One day as I was coming out of a beerhouse, and was about to go to see a friend, a policeman interfered with me. I became very impertinent to him, and he threatened in consequence to lock me up. I told him he would have a job to do that by himself. With that he got hold of me. I hit him a blow on the mouth, which he returned very severely with his staff. A fight then commenced—he, like a good soldier, standing up for his country. We fought till I was almost dead, tossing and rolling over in the dirt. I at length went with great violence to the ground, when, with the assistance of a man who came up at the moment, I was carried to the station-house. When we got there the man relaxed his hold of my legs, and I seized the collar of the policeman's coat, and tore the back clean out. This was only adding fuel to the fire, and multiplying the final consequences to myself. Next morning I was had up for trial, and was fined twenty shillings for striking the officer, and seven shillings for the damage done to his coat, or, in default of payment, one month's imprisonment. I said I would go to gaol willingly before I would give them one farthing. Whilst in the " cage," as I used to call it, in the court, I formed an acquaintance and palship with a friend, whom I met at the prison gates at the end of the month ; and I went with him " as an ox goeth to the slaughter, or as a bird hasteth to the snare, and knoweth not that it is for his life." With these companions I began to lead a worse life than before. I became so thoroughly reckless that I cared neither what I did nor whither I went.

My lot had now fallen among some of the professional thieves or "men of the day." But where are they now? All either gone to a felon's grave or inmates of a convict prison. I only of the lot am left to tell the story of the Cross, and of the goodness of God to an almost perishing sinner. Oh, how true are the words, " Rejoice, O young man, in the days of thy youth, and let thy heart cheer thee in the days of thy youth; but know this—for all these things God will bring thee into judgment." Could I have taken the advice which was so earnestly offered to me I should not have had thus to hold myself up as a warning to others of the danger they are in. Little did I think at one period of my life that I should become so blasted with infamy and crime as to be brought almost to the scaffold; and it is only " by the grace of God I am what I am " to-day. I knew very well I was doing wrong ; but every sinner out of Christ that is leading a similar course of life will never do better until the grace of God finds an entrance to the heart.

You may imagine, perhaps, dear reader, when you read these loving words, that my sin was at an end. But no, the worst has yet to come. I joined a gang of men who were as bad as myself, and with whom I went, for some length of time, to commit desperate crimes, being frequently brought up and discharged. One occasion I shall never forget. We went to break into a warehouse, but were disturbed by the police. They surrounded the place, and a desperate fight ensued. However, we all got clear off; but not before my poor head had been severely battered. Shortly after this my pals went to commit some great robbery ; they were caught, sent to the assizes, found guilty, and sentenced to penal servitude for a long period. This, it will no doubt be thought, ought to have caused me to turn from my evil course of life. But no; on I went as before. One day, whilst in drink, I thought of my poor dear mother. Although so steeped in sin there were times when I felt so unhappy as to be fit to take away the life of a fellow-creature should one lay hands upon me. Then thoughts of my dear mother would force themselves upon my mind, and I could not rest until I had found out her dwelling-place. On the occasion to which I refer I did so, and, what made matters worse, I was, as I said, in drink. I knew well that as soon as she saw me she would burst into tears, and the scene of that day will never be effaced from my memory. Not an hour had elapsed since she had been speaking of me. And, what with poverty and an almost broken heart, I found her looking pale and thin. Clasping me in her arms, she exclaimed, "Here's my son, my long-lost son!" And well might she so designate me, for when I last came out of prison no one knew whither I had gone. "Mother," I said, "you look very poorly." "Yes," she replied, "you have almost put me in the grave. But may God forgive thee my son; and I hope we shall meet in heaven." This was to me a severe trial; I could not restrain my tears. Down my mother fell upon her knees and prayed fervently to God to arrest me in my wicked career.

Thoughts of my latter end now began to trouble me, and these were the reflections that thrust themselves upon my mind: If my mother dies I shall have killed her—I shall have broken her heart! What will become of me then? I had almost become an outcast to all but my mother; her love for me was of that kind which never perishes. I knew that she was poor at this time, and as I had some money I offered it to her, but she refused its acceptance. "No," she said, "I will never eat the bread of idleness, nor yet will I be a partaker of dishonest gains." Then, turning to me, she exclaimed, "For my sake, for God's sake, and for your own sake, give up this life of sin and crime, or you will be the death of me." These words went to my heart like an arrow, and there they

B

stuck night and day until I was converted to God. The course of life I was pursuing. I knew would not last long; and there were moments, yea even when the drink demon was within me, that I suffered the severest pangs on account of my mother, and the advice I had neglected and despised; and I began to think that if there was one place in hell hotter than another it would be reserved for me, who had stumbled notwithstanding the advice I had received and the prayers offered up on my behalf. Nevertheless, I had become so hardened that, when reflection ceased, I cared for nothing but the course I was pursuing. I wanted to be a "trump"—a "man of the world." A "trump!" Yes, in good sooth I was one—that is taking the word as a nickname for a fool; for a fool I was, to all intents and purposes. Talking of nicknames reminds me that myself and companions gave such names to each other. They christened me "Curley," but if they had dubbed me "fool" the title would have fitted me much better.

On leaving my mother's house I promised her that I would do better; and for some time afterwards I went to see her daily, with the view of comforting her a little in her deep sorrow. I was at this time keeping company with some swellish individuals, and we used to frequent a dancing-room. I was always reckoned to be very quick with my hands, and now a new feature in my history became developed. After the dancing we were in the habit of adjourning to a private room, in which there was a set of boxing-gloves provided for the delectation of those who were inclined to have a turn at the "manly art" and become proficient in the science of self-defence. Our custom was to have a set-to with these young gents. Boxing, however, was not the only sport carried on in this room. Provision was also made for card playing, domino playing, and other modes of gambling; and these were indulged in not on week nights only but on Sunday evenings also. The son of the man who owned the place said to me, " Now, Harry, you can make a good thing out of the swells if you'll learn them the art of self-defence, for they are very anxious to learn." "Yes," thought I, "it *will* be a good thing for me, and there will be no fear of having to go to prison." I dreaded going there again, for I knew very well my fate would be transportation if I again appeared in the criminal's dock.

Accordingly, week after week I might be seen, on the good Sabbath-day, sparring with these swells, and a nice thing I made out of it too. I have come out of the place many a time with pounds in my pocket. Soon, however, this wickedness of the wicked came to an end. We could not at our gathering do without drink. The police were put upon the scent by seeing someone enter, and we were forced to give up the game. Nothing, then, would suit the parties I had been in the habit of meeting but making me into a fighting man. I was matched to fight for a small sum. Seconds were chosen, the time for the battle to come off arrived, and after a severe encounter I was proclaimed victor. This led to another match being made, the fight to come off in two months; and it occurred to me that if I only remained willing to indulge in this kind of work I was pretty certain of constant employment. The second battle I won also; and then on I went fighting and thieving for a long time; and those who are following a similar course to mine know very well that when they look upon a prize-fighter they behold a thief. For instance, one half of the battles won by these men are not fairly gained. This I know from experience. On one occasion, if the sponge had not been thrown up in my favour when it was I should have been beaten. Both sides go for the money, and with an equal determination not to be the losers. At length I began to think that this was the hardest work at which I had ever been engaged, and so there came upon me the inclination to give it up; and I did give it up, but only to enter upon something worse. I became acquainted with two men, strangers to me; and in a very short time I joined them in a most daring robbery. We got clear off with a pretty large booty, and began to spend the money very freely. I was in a vault drinking with my pals, and we had swallowed no less than six glasses of brandy each when I was under the necessity of going out into the street. Immediately I got there a tall man pushed against me. I asked him what he had done that for. The reply I got was a blow. So I " went into him," as the saying ran, right and left. He called out loudly, and soon I had some half-dozen on to me. I then called to my pals, and a desperate fight ensued. I retained a firm hold of my man, and in the struggle we both went bang through a window, carrying a portion of the frame along with us. I instantly jerked him back again, and he ran off. I then found that I had received a severe gash, two inches long, in the fleshy part of my hand, the mark of which I carry to this day, as a wound inflicted without justifiable cause. I was carried to a surgeon, who dressed the wound. I have often since looked at the mark and exclaimed, " This is a wound without cause." I am happy to say that the public-house in which I was drinking and the one opposite, through whose window I and my antagonist fell, have been closed by the magistrates. Would to God they would close the whole of them. These two have been the cause of many souls being lost. Often have I seen poor fallen girls who frequented there weeping outside at midnight, because they had no money wherewith to pay their lodgings. No one knows but God and those who have led a life like mine of the doings in these dens of infamy and crime. God grant that the reader of this book may never enter those horrible pits of vice, sin, and crime.

I was laid up for a time with my hand, and had to bear it in a sling. I knew not where to go nor what to do. Walking out one day I met an old friend, whom I went to reside with. All went right for a time; but I often accused myself whilst there of being once more in the house that leads to death and hell. Once I was a bright blooming lad—now I was a daring burglar, and an associate of thieves.

To show the reader how far a man can and will go when leading a life like this I insert the following: Living in a secret part of the town I became attached to some other men who were ready and willing to do anything. We entered together into a compact to break into a jeweller's shop, agreeing that if any of us were caught we would not inform of the others. Sunday, of all other days, was the day appointed for the commission of the deed. At the time appointed for the gang to meet I was at the rendezvous, but the others had not come up, and the scheme in consequence failed. This so enraged me that I swore I would have money before I slept, if I had to knock down and rob the first man I met to obtain it. I went to a public-house hard by, got drunk, and fell in with another man, who accompanied me the same night to carry out another daring robbery we had agreed to commit. On the way we encountered a young swell, with whom we entered into conversation, and being well dressed he had no suspicion as to the kind of persons he was talking with. He related to us how he had escaped being robbed of his watch and his money in a bad house. Little did he imagine that he had escaped the paw of the bear and fallen into that of a lion. Just as we were about to ease him of his cash and watch the police came upon us, and we had to beat a precipitate retreat. My pal then left me, saying he would go home, and I went back, moody with disappointment, to the public-house, and got more drink. It was then about ten o'clock. Shortly afterwards a man came in who, like myself, was a thief. In the bar parlour was a gentleman who was spending his money very freely. I thought it would be better in my hands than his. Yes, and I felt determined to have it, too. I called this friend of mine out, and proposed

to him that we should rob the gentleman and share the
spoil. To this he consented, and it was agreed that he
should hold him whilst I rifled his pockets. I then went
back into the house, and after we had been there about
fifteen minutes, the gentleman all the while squandering
his money upon all about him, I called him to the door,
and said, "Sir, you are in bad company; do you know
it?" Instantaneously my pal seized him, and held him
whilst I robbed him of his purse. We then made off, hid
the money, and returned to the public-house as if nothing
had happened, and, as though we were not conscious of
having done anything amiss, called for two glasses of
beer. The gentleman had gone to the police station to
give information of the robbery. In the house itself there
was considerable noise made about the affair, but we
swore that we knew nothing at all about it. In the
midst of the uproar the landlord called to the company
to "drink up," for it was closing time. I drank up my
beer, and just as I was saying "Good night, all," on my
way out, the detectives and the man who had been
robbed met me. "Stop," said one of the policemen;
"don't be in a hurry to go." Then, addressing the
gentleman, he asked him if he could identify any person
present who had been concerned in the robbery. The
man looked round, failed to recognise my associate, but
pointing towards me, cried out, "That's the man that
called me out and robbed me." The police then seized
hold of me. I was not for going quietly, and so they
began to handcuff me. I declared that if I had to go
they would have to carry me; and this they did, feeling,
no doubt, that they had got a good case. On reaching
the station house, the man said he did not wish to prose-
cute if he could get back his purse and money, for in the
former was something of no use whatever to any person
but the owner. The police, however, informed him that
I was one of a gang of daring burglars, and ordered him
to attend at the court the following morning at ten

o'clock. I was searched, but nothing was found upon me. It is not for me to describe here how the business was managed; suffice it to say that the gentleman got back his purse and money, under a promise that he would leave the town; and when I was brought up for trial no prosecutor appeared, and I was discharged.

Shortly after this affair had blown over I was engaged in a most daring exploit, in which we had to face a desperate struggle, in the course of which I received a frightful wound in my head; but I managed, nevertheless, to escape, losing blood at every step I took, and in a strange place. I was obliged to seek surgical aid, and was asked how the wound had been inflicted. I, with a lie in my mouth, although so near to death, said I was going along a back street, when a man and his wife were quarrelling, and just as I was passing the man came running at his wife with a knife to stab her, and stabbed me instead. "Well," said the doctor, "had you been five minutes later you would have lost your life." These, dear reader, were wounds without cause, and as long as I live I shall never forget them. I was now forced to leave the den of thieves and seek a shelter in my mother's home. I found her pale as death, but the moment she saw me she clasped me in her arms, exclaiming, "My son, my son, I heard you were killed." "Not killed, mother," I said, "but almost; I am almost dead; and it is much but I have come home to die." My poor mother wept, and gently but earnestly reminded me of the counsel she had given me, and entreated that, whilst there was time, I should repent, forsake my wicked ways, and give myself to God. I felt the full force of her entreaty, and promised that if I got better I would lead a different life. But oh, how this, like all my previous resolutions, melted away! I got better, plunged deeper and deeper into sin and crime, and the last was worse than the first. I became associated with burglars of a worse type than any I had previously known, and we all went to live to-

gether. I took a house for the purpose of hiding plunder
and ill-gotten gains. This was veritably the house that
led to hell; and although I was fully conscious that I was
doing wrong I still pursued the downward path. But
my sand-glass had now almost run out. I took another
house for the purpose of deceiving the police, and many
were the daring robberies committed. On one occasion
we were caught at our nefarious work; the people and the
police surrounded the house. We were on a wall at the
time, and one of my companions was taken. I stood
there, with an iron bar in my hand, and was so afraid of
being taken that, in a fit of desperation, I swore I would
fell the first man who laid hands upon me. Jumping
from the wall to the ground, I took to my heels, was
pursued, but managed to escape. Justice, however,
followed me, crying out, as it were, "Thus far shalt thou
go, but no further." And as I am quite tired of dealing
with the dark side of my life, I will relate one more
incident and then conclude.

Before doing so, will you allow me, dear reader, whether
young or old, to ask you a question? Have you a mother?
If so, you will remember the time, no doubt, when she
first taught you to clasp your hands together, and say—

Gentle Jesus, meek and mild,
Look upon a little child.

How sweet the memory of those days! My mother!
What happy reminiscences pass through the mind at the
sound of these words! Do not say you forget those
happy times, though you may now be a hardened sinner.
It may be you have followed that best of earthly friends
to the grave; but you well remember her last words—
they have rung in your ears many a time—"Bless my
lads! My son, my daughter, meet me in heaven!" Did
not the silent tear drop on the coffin as you saw her
remains lowered into the grave! Forsaken by all friends,
and left to corruption, to mingle with the dust, that
mother's soul is now in glory. Can you forget her,

reader? I say you cannot. The memory of that mother still abides in your affections, though you may be one of the greatest sinners that ever lived. More especially, as you gaze upon a portrait on the wall of your cottage, though it is faded, you can clearly see the face and form it represents, and you are led to exclaim—"My mother!" Can you think about her? Can you look at her without remembering what she taught you to say in the days of your youth? "Gentle Jesus," &c.; "My son, meet me in heaven." Remember, dear reader, ere long your eyes that look upon these pages will become dim, your body will become a pale, cold corpse; for "it is appointed unto man once to die, but after this the judgment." How are you living? Are you following that mother's precepts, or are you pursuing the evil way of sinners? If so, "be sure your sin will find you out." Oh, how awful will it be for you to find yourself in hell, after the counsel and advice you have received! Let me ask you, reader, to examine yourself, before you read another line of this book. Am I prepared to die? Die you must; that is certain, but uncertain when it will come. Go, then, to your mother's friend, Jesus Christ, the Saviour of sinners. I do not ask you whether you are like what I was. You need not be as bad as that to go to hell. Oh, no! You have an immortal soul. That soul has been purchased by no less a price than the precious blood of Jesus; and as long as you keep it back from God you have no part nor lot in the matter of that inheritance which is laid up for the children of God. Can you bear, then, the racking reflection of your dear mother being in heaven, and yourself thrust out? Let me ask you, then, whose fault will it be if you don't get to heaven?

The great reason why I have mentioned your mother is because experience is a good teacher. I have suffered intense agony in the prison cell on account of disobeying my mother's counsel; and I can safely say the magnetic power of my mother's prayers have haunted me night and day. They echoed through the walls of the prison cell: "Harry give thy heart to God, and all will yet be well." Mothers, do you ever pray for your children? Mine prayed for me for years. She had that faith that God commends: faith that will not take a denial. Read Gospel of St. Matthew, xv., 22, 28. She prayed like Jacob did. "Bless the lads—especially Harry." God heard her prayer,

And saved me though I did rebel ;
My Jesus has done all things well.

Pray on, mothers and fathers, and do not shut the doors of your hearts against your prayers. Do not say, like some mothers who have prodigals going astray, "I will leave no door open by which the wayward child can return." Do not do this. The door of mercy is not closed against you, and why should you close your heart and door against your child? Many a poor wandering son or daughter would have found their way back again to the parental roof if the door had been left open. Read Gospel of St. Luke, xv: "Forgive, and ye shall be forgiven." My mother loved me though I was a wicked man ; and just at the time when I was in my hottest rage of sin she prayed for me. I had been some time away from her, but not without hearing how she was breaking her heart on my account. At the time I refer to my mother was forced to leave my cruel stepfather for his brutality to her. At this time she had three little children by him. I, of course, had grown up to be a man ; in fact, I had been such, in my own estimation, for a long time.

On one occasion I was asked to accompany others into a certain beerhouse, to play at dominoes and cards. (Working men, these are the devil's toys.) While I was playing who should come in but my stepfather. He called for a glass of beer (I must tell you he liked it), and then began abusing my mother with foul language. I will give you the scene—not boastingly—for I have a reason for so doing. I went on with my game, and took no notice of him. The last I heard of him was that he was beating my dear mother; and I remembered when I was a boy—when he turned me into the street, and beat my mother for taking me in—telling him if ever I lived to grow up I should not forget him. I may just say here, on the day prior to my discharge from prison, the first time I was sentenced, one of the principal officers wrote to him to say he must receive me or they would see him about it. He did let me enter the house at the time, but before the day was over he began to abuse my mother, referring to me—" Look at your son; what will he become?" Then he turned me out into the street. It was at this time I uttered the above. All the time I was playing at dominoes he was cursing at my mother, although she was not there. Jumping up from my seat, I seized him and tumbled him into the street. He went and fetched a policeman, and gave me in charge. When the policeman was about to take me to the station-house I said, "Stay, my friend, 'one story's good till another's told.'" I called him friend. Of course I was a good customer to the police; but at this time they had not seen me for some time, nor had hold of me either. The policeman kept a firm hold of me, when I said, " Look here, Mr. P., allow me to tell you a true tale. Have you ever seen a poor woman weeping at midnight on your beat at any of these corners? If you have, that is my poor mother. This man that has given me in charge is my stepfather. He has, I may safely say, been the means of my ruin. He has nearly killed my mother many a time, turned her out of doors, and of course she had nowhere to go. I have got into prison more than once." I here swore if I had my will with him I would kill him. When the policeman heard my tale he relaxed his hold, and told me to tell mother to get a warrant for his apprehension for his brutality to her. This was not done; mother took the three little children with her and left him. God opened her a way, and though years have passed away she has stuck to the children, but has never lived with him since. My prayers, and mother's too, are that God will convert his soul. After all his treatment to both of us we do forgive him, and long to see him happy. Should one of these books fall into his hands, I hope, when he thinks of the past, like Peter, he will weep, and come to that Saviour who took poor Harry, the outcast, in, and pardoned all his sins, and made him happy in His forgiving love.

Reader, are you a stepfather or stepmother? Be kind to the children whom you have taken charge of. Remember there is a day coming which shall reveal all things; and how dreadful it will be if your children rise up in judgment to condemn you. This need not be. Fathers, mothers, sons, and daughters, listen to the loving words of Jesus—"Come unto me, all ye that labour and are heavy laden, and I will give you rest."

The reader must not be surprised to hear, though I had a strong affection for my mother, yet I had not embraced my mother's God, or given up my evil companions. I was always afraid of the iron grasp of the law, and very unhappy.

By this time I had become a confirmed drunkard, but I went to see my dear mother. I am sorry to say I was in a state of intoxication. At the first sight of her, I shall never forget, she burst into tears, and earnestly entreated me to consider my ways, and be wise before it was too late. I well knew and still know "the way of transgressors is hard," for "God shall wound the head of his enemies, and the hairy scalp of such an one as goeth on still in his trespasses," and if I went to hell it would be my own fault. Here my dear mother told me that my sin would find me out, and I should think of her words when it was too late. "Yes, Harry," said my mother, "you are a fool to yourself. Don't break my heart, Harry, by going on in sin, for if anything happens to you

again you will sure to be transported; 'then shall ye
bring down my grey hairs with sorrow to the grave.'"
I wept; and I can safely say, with all my heart, had
I my life to live over again, I would start from the Cross,
with Christ in my heart. After promising my mother I
would do better I left her; but, like many more, the
glaring gaslight in the public-house had too much charm
for me—drink, drink, drink I would have. No sooner
had I lost sight of my mother's counsel and advice than
I was as bad as ever.

Shortly after the last affray my male companions were
transported, and I was alone. And, oh, had I but language to convey to you, dear reader, an idea of the
feeling which I experienced when I looked back upon my
past life! An old companion of mine, just emerged from
prison, found me out, and we agreed to pursue our career
together, and to have but one purse. For a time we
prospered in our sinful business; but how true it is that
"the pitcher may often go to the well, yet it is sure to
be broken in the end!" I went with others to commit a
robbery, but we were detected and pursued. I was
stopped by a young man, but, breaking away from his
grasp, I vowed that if he dared to follow me I would put
a knife into him. "Stop thief!" was the cry raised after
me, and after a severe struggle I was captured, and safely
lodged in the station-house. Next day I was taken before
the magistrates, a formidable black sheet was displayed
against me, and I was sent for trial. Whilst in prison
my mother visited me, and as long as I live I shall never
forget what she said to me. On the day of my trial she
was in the court and in tears. I employed Mr. Torr to
plead for me; but all in vain. After a trial of eight
hours I was found guilty of housebreaking. At the
sound of the word guilty my eyes sank in my head, my
jaw quivered, and I shook from head to foot. My poor
mother had dropped for dead in the court, and, with open
arms, I cried for mercy, not on my account, but for the

sake of her whose heart had yearned towards me throughout my entire career. "Deal leniently with you!" said the judge: "No; I shall send you where you ought to have been years ago. The sentence upon you is that you be kept in penal servitude for seven years." What I felt on that miserable night when removed from the dock to the prison cell, and what my poor mother must have felt, I must leave you, dear reader, to imagine; for words would fail me were I to attempt a description.

It might be supposed that I had now turned; but, ah, no! something more dreadful still remained behind. One of the officers of the prison reported me for making signs in the yard, and I was put on bread and water. Whilst in the cell the devil reigned in my heart; and I swore that if that officer ever came into the cell whilst I was there I would have his life. I had made up my mind that as soon as he entered I would seize him, and throw him over the rails from the top landing. Being one of the taskmasters I went up to him one day in the exercise-yard, and asked him if he would be so kind as to come to my cell, for I did not know how to do my work, intending when he came to take his life. I was determined to do no more work until he did come, and I stuck to my determination. For two weeks my wicked heart was breathing out threatenings against him. A few days after this I went to exercise, the same officer being in charge of the prisoners in the yard. I was not doing right in his estimation, when he called out, "Now, Seven (that was my number), mind what you're at again." I ran up to him in a great rage, and said, "Do you know what Seven has got? Seven has got seven years, and if you don't let me alone I'll make it hot for you." I then passed on, expecting to be brought before the governor, but I was not. I had frightened the man. Time passed on, and one day he came to my cell and unlocked the door. I was just thinking about him at the moment, and rose from my stool in a rage, but he stepped back, and said, "Seven, you are a fool to yourself, getting punished for your own self-will." I was struck to the earth as it were, and, instead of carrying out my wicked purpose, I listened to him ; and, oh, dear reader, suddenly, as if by a miracle, the lion was turned into a lamb. The words of my dear mother sounded in my ears, and I cried for mercy. The man left me ; and, oh, how I wept ! Directly afterwards I was sent for to go below into the governor's office. When I got there Mr. Wright, the prison philanthropist, was waiting to see me at the request of my mother. By the power of his words he soon melted me to tears. He repeated to me the 51st Psalm, and assured me that if I insisted upon having my own way in prison I should have to suffer. He pointed me to that God I had so long despised and neglected. He spoke to me of my mother's sorrow, and recommended me to Jesus ; and that, though I had gone so far in iniquity, I could yet find mercy if I would seek for it. He said much more, and what he said went direct to my heart. On retiring to my cell the Bible, for the first time for years, was opened at the 51st Psalm. After I had read it and the first six verses of the 52nd Psalm, I felt as if my heart would have broken. The next day, being Sunday, I went to chapel, and heard a sermon from the text, Hebrews xii., 17. It made such an impression upon my mind that I became almost mad to think that I should only give the very dregs of my life to that Saviour who had striven with me so long ; and God and myself only know what I felt. I was so deeply under conviction that at night I could not sleep. Morning came, and I was miserable, sorrowing without hope and without God in the world. Often did I cry out in agony of soul, " Lord, save me ; I perish." I thought I heard my mother's voice outside the prison walls, saying, " O Harry, give your heart to God, and all will yet be well." I asked myself the question, " What profit have I in those things whereof I am now ashamed?" I looked back to the days that had gone, and noted how I had stumbled notwithstanding prayers, advice, and the Spirit of God striving with me. I was visited by my mother, and returned to my cell more wretched than ever, for something was sounding in my ears, "Too late! too late!" But what I knew taught me better than to listen to the devil about its being too late. I had been taught that God could and would save to the uttermost; that whosoever will may come; and that included me. I was deep in reflection; and whilst, like the Prodigal Son when feeding on the husks, looking back to former days, and thinking of my mother and my home, I composed the following lines :—

Was there a time when peaceful light
And joys of home were my delight?
Was there a time when all was fair,
And I had neither grief nor care?
But have those pleasures vanish'd quite?
Are days no longer beaming bright?
Why is this fearful change come o'er
And why is peace not as before?
'Twas sin, that bane of every joy—
Sin, that can wither, blight, destroy.
Sin triumphed, and I left my God,
The paths of wickedness I trod;
And now in grief I bow my head,
For joys are gone, and peace is fled.
But stay: is all now sad and drear?
Doth no glad ray of hope appear?
Forbid it heaven! I see afar
The blessed beam of Bethlehem's star;
I hear a still small voice proclaim,
In softening tones, the Saviour's name:
And, hark! methinks it seems to say—
"My blood can wash your sins away;
My love can heal your wandering heart;
My power can still new life impart."

And, blessed be God! I became endowed with new life, and the once hardened sinner began to cry for mercy. A new light shone in my heart, and I felt the load fall therefrom. That night I wrestled with God, and ere I closed my eyes in sleep I found that Saviour whom I had so long neglected and despised; and to-day I can sing—

Although afflictions were severe,
In mercy they were sent;
They have stopped the prodigal's career,
And forced him to repent.

I was happy now, and whatsoever I did prospered. I

became deeply concerned about my younger brother's salvation. I wrote to him, entreating him to give his heart to God, and to shun the public-house, lest he should be brought to the same place of punishment as myself. I need only say that my brother did give his heart to God and renounced the public-house, and from that day to this he has been travelling Zionwards.

I did not remain long in the Manchester prison; I was sent off to Wakefield, Yorkshire. In this prison I was put to mat weaving. I was so filled with the love of God that I felt as if I could shout Hallelujah to everybody I saw. I shall never forget one time as I sat in the chapel, the poor prisoner that sat next to me said, " How long have you got?" I said, " Seven years." " Oh, dear me," he replied, " I have got three years—never was in prison before in my life." " Sorry for you," said I. He then told me he had got his punishment for stealing sheep. I said, " Well, my friend, the best thing you can do is to give your heart to God. He has saved me; He will save you and make you happy. When you get back to your cell go down upon your knees and ask God to save you. I will pray for you too." I need only say that the next day we were both brought up and put upon bread and water for talking in chapel; and, praise the Lord! though on bread and water, I could sing and pray to Him who had delivered me from the prison of sin. Here in this cell I knelt and prayed that God would save my fellow-prisoner in the next cell. We were both praying after midnight so much that the officer knocked at the cell door and told us to be quiet; but, like Paul and Silas, we sang praises unto our God. The light of heaven beamed upon my next-door neighbour's soul, and before the morning he could say that God had saved his soul. We were both happy in Jesus, and as long as I remained in that prison I often comforted him by telling him that Christ would keep him safe, and then even the prison would seem a palace to him. I

c

was sorry when I had to leave him, for after my separate confinement I was called up to go to Portland Convict Prison, and here I was not ashamed of the Gospel of Christ, for it had been the power of God unto my salvation. I had to associate with all classes of men, and suffered great persecution because I loved the Lord Jesus. But I was not daunted thereby. I had tried both sides of a prison—the inside and the outside—and, come what would, I was not to be moved. I remembered the words, "Blessed are they which are persecuted for righteousness' sake, for theirs is the kingdom of heaven."

After I had been in Portland for a while, I was called up to write a farewell letter home prior to my departure to Gibraltar, in answer to which I received a letter from my mother, which made me light-hearted. My once broken-hearted parent was now happy, because I was happy in Jesus. "Thank God," she said to me, "I have lived to see my son Harry converted to God. Since you left I have never ceased to pray for you night and day, and now I can die, crying—

> Above the rest this note shall swell—
> My Saviour hath done all things well."

I tried as much to comfort her, as I had previously caused her sorrow, by writing to her as often as the prison rules would allow, and that was once every three months.

We sailed from Portland for the hulks at Gibraltar on the 27th of May, 1863, and landed in June. As long as I live the name of Gibraltar will cling to my memory. What with the work and heat we had to endure I did not think I should have lived. But I put my trust in God, who had done for me more than language can describe. I was sent to labour in the stone-quarry for a time; then I was put to my own trade. All went on as well as I could expect in this life, notwithstanding that I had to put up with a deal of abuse from my fellow-prisoners—now and then, however, meeting with a few that loved the Lord. We formed a Bible-class, the Scripture-reader superintending it; and our meetings, which were held once a week, were as a well of water to my soul. I also joined the singing-class, the members of which had to sing in church, and this added to my happiness. One anthem which we were set to learn delighted me much; the words were taken from the parable of the Prodigal Son: " For this my son was dead, and is alive again, he was lost and is found." I again wrote home, and received a comforting letter in return. I had also a book sent to me by my brother, called " The Last of the Patriarchs." On one of the fly-leaves was inscribed the following lines of poetry, which my brother had written as being appropriate to my position :—

> Far away from mother's home,
>     Though in exile you are kept,
> Though your mind may often roam,
>     Dear brother, do not fret.
>
> Look to God, your heavenly Father,
>     He will make you happy yet ;
> Now his praise and mercy gather,
>     Dear brother, do not fret.
>
> Though the world may scoff and taunt you,
>     Jesu's mercy don't forget ;
> Though the very demons taunt you,
>     Dear brother, do not fret.
>
> When you gaze upon our faces,
>     Let not your tears in sorrow flow ;
> Think of heaven's happy places,
>     Prepare thyself that thou may go.
>
> If ne'er on earth we meet again,
>     Let us cleave to Christ, and sing,
> And in that land of pleasure reign
>     With our immortal King.
>
> Good-bye, dear brother, for a time—
>     Thy liberty will tell ;
> Soon that sweet liberty be thine—
>     Farewell, dear Harry, farewell.

The following are the words of advice which my mother sent me in regard to this book :—

Dear Harry,—Read this book with delight: it will teach you to be happy, holy, and contented. Confidently assured how God takes care of all who trust in Him, you will, in some parts of it, read what you experience. It will always be new to you, and bear reading : showing you the hand of God in everything. Nothing happens by chance ; there is no sorrow, grief, or pain but is seen by His eye, however lonely the spot, however remote.

In 1865 the cholera broke out in the prison, and made

fearful ravages among the inmates. Daily, convicts who were well one hour were dead the next, so sudden and so fatal were the attacks of the remorseless epidemic. I was at length seized with it myself, and thought I was going to die; and as I lay in the hospital among the dying and the newly-dead, the scene was truly awful, and the groans which broke upon the ear cutting to the very soul. In conversation with the doctor I expressed my belief that, after all, I was not going to die, for I felt conscious that God had a work for me to do. And in this belief I was right, for I recovered; and to God be all the glory.

As a warning to scoffers I give the particulars of a case that came under my own observation. One convict, who had been sentenced to six years' penal servitude, said, whilst the cholera was raging, that he did not care for it —that it was only those who frightened themselves with it that died. He cursed and swore fearfully. He was shortly afterwards seized with the disease, and in two hours, after a heavy oath had passed his lips, he was a corpse. Sinner, scoffer, prepare to meet thy God.

I will not enter into a minute history of my prison life, which, after much suffering, came to a close. After a hard struggle of five years and seven months I was sent to Millbank Prison, Westminster, there to await my discharge by the order of the Secretary of State, and on the 4th of September, 1867, I was sent home to my friends. My brother, who had been converted through my instrumentality, wrote to me requesting me to come to him. I did so, trusting in God to open a way for me, and was not disappointed. I got work, and all went on well for some time, the light of prosperity beaming upon my path. I joined a religious class, attended band meetings and prayer meetings; and many times when relating what God had done for me I saw that good was done to others.

Having been so long away from my mother I was in great distress as to how I should present myself before her. I went to Manchester, and resolved to send my brother into the house first, as a kind of pioneer, to warn her not to be troubled, for I was nigh at hand, and should be with her in about ten minutes. When I entered the house, this was my salutation—" Praise God for what he has done to me !" My mother burst into tears, and all in the house were similarly affected. " Let us pray," I said, and we all knelt down ; and I, in a fervent prayer, returned thanks to God for my providential deliverance from sin and death, and for the happy change which I had experienced. The news soon spread that Harry had come home, and that he was praying. First one and then another came into the house ; and many hearts thanked God for what they heard and saw.

I soon became well known, and was sent for to many places to relate my experience and to recount the story of the wonderful change God had wrought in my heart. On these occasions I have seen the poor drunkard, with his bloodshot eyes, resolve at once to abandon drink and to give his heart to God ; the wife-beater, who had been a terror to his household, melted into tears, and go home a new creature in Christ Jesus ; the thief, who, like myself, had been often in prison for outraging the laws of his country, at once renounce his evil deeds and become an honest man ; and the blasphemer, the wicked Bible-despiser and Christ-rejecter induced to seek mercy, and, happily, to find it. For a long time I have prayed that God would use me for His glory and for the salvation of sinners. I have also prayed much for my old companions, who are yet in the broad path of ruin. May God save them ere they perish, as He has graciously saved me !

Dear reader, if you are a thief, let me ask you, as a friend that loves you and your soul's salvation, what have you gained by your crimes, from the moment you set out to the present hour, but shame, and dread, and fear, and a fearful looking-for of judgment and fierce indignation from God ? " What shall it profit a man if he gain the whole world and lose his own soul?" I never knew happiness till I found Christ. Hear, poor thief, the words of the Saviour: "Let him that stole steal no more." Remember, "all that's got by thieving turns to sorrow, shame, and pain." Read the 23rd chapter of St. Luke's Gospel, reflect upon it, and may God have mercy upon you and save you! Do I address a poor drunkard, drowning his senses in that which will finally damn him? God has declared that no drunkard can enter the kingdom of heaven. Let him take courage. I was once as bad as he; but the Lord—bless His holy name!—has brought me through. And oh, let me, dear reader, whoever you may be, persuade you not to despise this book. The man who is now warning you has been as near to hell as anyone out of it; and I can say from my heart it is a blessed truth that when a man becomes so depraved that even his fellowmen cast him off, God in His mercy will accept the very dregs of his life, and build them up into a fabric of beauty—a monument of his loving-kindness and infinite goodness.

I shall never forget the day when Jesus washed my sins away—I am now called into the vineyard of the Lord, to work for His glory and the salvation of sinners. I hope God will spare my life, that I may be useful in the cause of the Cross, for I know that they who win souls are wise, and "he that converteth a sinner from the error of his ways shall hide a multitude of sins." Since I became a new man in Christ I have been to all parts of the country, bearing the reproach, despising the shame, that I might win souls; and many men and poor fallen women, too, have I seen renounce their wicked ways and flee to that Saviour who turns none away. None need despair: "Ho, everyone that thirsteth, come ye to the waters, without money and without price." Look at me: am I not a brand plucked out of the fire? Jesus, the sinner's friend, who sticketh closer than a brother, has, thank God, been a friend to me; He has never left me nor forsaken me. At this time I was asked to hold services amongst the Pendleton workpeople. Many professed to find that Saviour whom they had set at naught, neglected, and despised. Many homes that were miserable through drink and sin are now made happy in the Lord. I have visited most of them, and have seen for myself that the change has been real. For example, I will cite one case, and if it were only for this my labours have not been in vain in the Lord. One night myself and some of the brethren connected with the hall in which our meetings were held were out in the streets singing—

> There is a fountain filled with blood,
>   Drawn from Emmanuel's veins;
> And sinners, plunged beneath that flood,
>   Wash out their guilty stains;

also giving invitations to all to come, the seats being free, and no collection. At the close of the meeting I saw a man much broken down, with his arm in a sling. I spoke to him encouragingly of Jesus. He said he was a wicked man, and, pointing to his arm, added, " This is through drink; but I cannot stop now; I am in pain with my hand and the life I have led." He promised, however, that he would come again the next night. He kept his word. I told the simple story of the Cross and what God had done for me. Whilst in the midst of the service the poor prodigal came forward and sought and obtained mercy. The next day I went to see him. He related to me the more striking passages of his career; how he had been a soldier, and guarded the very prison at Gibraltar in which I had been confined; and how for a long time he had gone recklessly on " sowing wild oats." " But," exclaimed he, " thank God, I will now be different." He then told me what was the matter with his hand, and this is the man's own story: " I had been drinking for some time, and my wife had determined to leave me, and we made the agreement. I then left her, went to the public-house, got more drink, and at night in a rage swore

I would 'do for her.' The doors being fastened, I went to the back window, and whilst attempting to get through to carry out my wicked intention I fell with my arm through the glass and injured my hand. Thus I failed in my violent purpose." And what a mercy! The man is now a new creature in Christ Jesus, and happy with his wife. "Old things have passed away; behold, all things have become new." Dear reader, are you yet in sin? If so, there is mercy for you—

> While the lamp holds out to burn
> The vilest sinner may return.

But if you put off the opportunity, "how shall you escape if you neglect so great a salvation?"

Here is another case which came under my own observation, which I cite as a warning to those who may be putting off the day of grace. A young woman who came one night to our service was strongly convinced that she was a sinner; but, alas! the word did not take deep root; she went away unsaved. A few days afterwards, I was told, she got into the hands of the police, and when in the cell she fell to weeping. Another unfortunate in the place inquired what she was crying for. "Oh," was the reply, "had I but taken warning from what I heard spoken the other night I should not have been in this miserable place." Dear reader, one false step may plunge you into destruction. Let me urge you, then, to be in earnest in your search after the pearl of great price—the one thing needful—which is able to save your souls.

After many blessings at Pendleton, I went to hold special services in Eccles. Many of the working classes were gathered together through the exertions of Mr. John Sugden, of that place, whose sympathy with the people had great weight; others of the place assisting. We commenced our labour in the open-air, and one feature which presented itself there is worthy of notice. As we stood on the waste, preaching Christ, a passer-by said to a brother that was giving out tracts—"Can you tell me that man's name that's preaching on the bank?" "Henry Holloway," was the reply. "Well, I never! If that man's preaching about Jesus I'll go home, and come no more to Eccles Wakes" (it then being Eccles Wakes).

It was suggested by Mr. Sugden that a thorough mission should take place, in visiting the people's houses, and compelling them to come in, that the Lord's house might be filled. Accordingly we set off, assisted by not a few who voluntarily came forward to work for Jesus, some of whom had just been converted. I was going along one street accompanied by Mr. Sugden, when we came to a standstill under a public-house window, in which I heard sounds of revelry (it was Sunday, about two o'clock). My heart yearned to go in. I had been a champion in the devil's service, why not for Christ? In I went. The landlord was just going to the cellar to draw some beer, when I went in and said: "My dear working-men, will you allow me to have a word with you about Christ?" I said I was a working-man myself, and knew the feelings of every one of them. I made short work of telling them what God had done for me. The words went home to some of their hearts, for not a man touched his glass the whole time I was in. The landlord was in the cellar drawing beer, and whether he was tapping a fresh barrel or not I cannot tell, but I had time to say a good deal. Mr. Sugden, seeing I was a long time, came in, and spoke a kindly word about Jesus to them. When Mr. Landlord came out of the cellar with the orders, "What's this?" he said. "Are you going to make my house into a chapel?" and, tapping me on the shoulder, said, "Young fellow, you must go out of my house; this is not the place to preach about Christ?" This went to my heart, and I said, "Oh, my dear working men, do you hear that? Would you like to die here, where Christ is not fit to be mentioned? Working men, if Christ is not fit to be named here in this taproom it is not a fit place for you; come out; outside is the best and safest side ; and if you do love that beer of yours so much that you cannot leave it, bring it with you into the street, and I will preach the Gospel to you there." I need only say that several came to hear the Gospel, and were greatly blessed.

After I left a large tea-meeting was held, at which six hundred were present ; Mr. William Birch, jun., presiding. On the platform were ministers from different churches, all of whom expressed their thanks to Almighty God for what he had done in Eccles.

I am thankful to say they have also opened a British Workman, where the working man can go and sit, and read, and think—all are welcome ; but they cannot be supplied with drink, such as pale ale, bitter beer, Allsop's, and stout.

A word to you, reader. Has it not made you pale many a time ? Has it not made that dear wife of yours pale, and children, too ? Has it not put bitterness into your domestic happiness ? Oh, yes. Stout ; yes it is stout—it makes fat churchyards ; it makes hell fuller every day, and yet there is room. Reader, wilt thou take my advice ? Do not let the glaring gaslight in the public-house attract thee, but let thy wife and sons at home amuse thee. The bright fire in the taproom may have a charm for thee— it had for me—but if thou will take my advice and keep thy money thou canst have a good fire at home. I pray that, while you are reading this, the Holy Ghost will light up a pathway in your soul, and lead you on to heaven. If this book should fall into the hands of one that denies that the Gospel is the power of God unto salvation, let me show you a case in the same place before referred to. I was preaching in one of the schoolrooms there, assisted by a dear brother in the Gospel bonds. On his return home after the meeting he had to go through a lonely spot ; and, unfortunately, he suffered sometimes after speaking with dizziness in the head. At this time it seized him. He was compelled to sit down on some steps, when two very rough-looking men came up, laid hold of him, demanding his money, to which he replied, "I have none; do not hurt a servant of God, will you?" "Oh, good, ———!" cried one of the men, "loose him; this man preaches the Gospel along with Holloway." Here they let go their hold, and said they were both sorry for what they had done. They had got so reduced in circumstances through sin they were compelled to rob or starve, for no one would employ them. The man begged of them to go home with him. They were afraid at first, but afterwards went. This poor but Christian man gave them a supper, such as he had. After supper he said, "Let us pray." He prayed that, if it pleased God, he would open a way for those two men. The tear was seen to fall. They went home. He promised to see a gentleman about them, and meet them next day at a certain time; but, strange to say, instead of meeting them, two females came, and, seeing him waiting about, asked him was he the person that was accosted the night before by two men. "Yes," was the reply. "Well, do you know, one of those men is my brother. This morning, at a certain time, his old master came to our house, and promised to reinstate him in his old employment, if he would be sober and honest."

Dear reader, can you account for this? If not, I can. What did one say when about to use brutality to the man? Did not they see something in that man that belonged to Christ? "Let him alone; he has been preaching the Gospel along with Harry." They were evidently afraid of Harry's God—Harry's Saviour. True it must be they had either heard me preach, or heard what God had done for me; and, like St. Paul the apostle, when he was going to Damascus to persecute the Christians, God stopped him in his mad career.

Shortly after this I went and took my stand in one of our Manchester markets. I hired a table, for which I paid threepence, and a shilling for toll. I rang my Gospel bell, then I sang my little song—"Come, ye that fear the Lord." This was a new feature here. I was surrounded on the right hand and on the left with auctioneers, quack doctors, &c. Several hundred people listened with great attention. I began by saying—"My dear working men and women, I am a native of this town, of which some of you well know. It is no new thing I have to tell you. I have been a convict, but by the grace of God I have put on the new man. On this very spot where I stand I have revelled in sin; in yonder slaughter-houses (pointing to the public-houses) my voice has often been heard in the drunkard's song; but to-day, praise God, 'I am not ashamed of the Gospel of Christ, for it is the power of God unto salvation unto everyone that believeth.'" Here I stood for two hours, boldly preaching Christ and him crucified. I was interrupted by a man in the crowd, who shouted out—"I never heard a man like you in my life; that sounds logic; but, after all, will your preaching remove the marks from my flesh?" I cried out—"Has Satan been whipping thee, lad? He's a bad master; he has whipped me. See," pointing to my head, in which I had an old wound without cause. "Here's another, my friend [showing him my hand, the gash received, before alluded to]; my back, too, has felt the whip: these are all telling me 'the way of transgressors is hard.' God has converted my soul; the brand of sin has gone from my heart, but still the marks are here, on my head, hand, &c. What marks have you got, my friend?" "Marks!" the man cried out. "The devil has burnt them in me here." The man, before several hundred people, showed his flesh, and in his side was the brand, in large letters, "B.C.," representing bad character. This he got in the army, and a sentence of seven years' penal servitude. I said, "You want to know whether my preaching will remove the marks? No, it will not." Pointing to a quack doctor that stood not far from me, recommending his pills for all manner of diseases, blotches on the skin, face, &c.,

I said, "Do you hear that man ? He says he can cure any disease." He replied, " Yes, I hear him." I said, "There is a mighty disease which neither he nor any other earthly physician can cure ; and you have it, my friend ; it has given you those brands. It is sin ; and if you will come to Christ, the great physician of sin-sick souls, he will remove the brand of sin from your heart, and then you will not require any more marks from man. God help you, my brother !" Many wept along with the poor man with the brand. "I'll go home," he said, "and take your advice." Surely God saved his soul. I left the ground with a kindly shake of the hand from many a working-man, and a " God bless you." As I was going away I was followed by a man in tears. Never in my life did I see a man cry like him ; and, putting up his hand, he cried—" I ought to be hung, I ought to be hung." " For what ?" I said. "To see and hear a man like you preaching the Gospel." I looked at the man and said, " Don't I know you?" "You ought to do ; I have been near enough to you." Reader, this very man was no other than one of the convicts that was chained to my leg when we left the City Prison for Wakefield ; in fact, the very man that was fastened to my right side. How he wept ? I wanted my tea very badly, but I knew the Lord's work must be done. When Christ travelled to Samaria to save a poor woman, ought I not take my brother by the hand ? I took him to a room where I knew there was a meeting held (experience). We began to sing. I passed the word to the minister who was conducting the meeting to turn it into one for prayer. This being done, I got my friend down on his knees : he wept and cried for mercy : the Lord broke his hard heart and healed it again with the balm of Gilead. Praise the Lord for such a rich blessing to accompany my labour in that market-place ! This was the first time I had been there with the Gospel; it was not the last, for I presented myself for weeks, weather permitting, and much good was done in the name of the Lord.

I was then called to labour at Oldham in connection with Mr. and Mrs. Streets, who have been superintending work for the Lord for some years. God has honoured the labours of these zealous workers for Christ. They sent for me. I went, and here I had the unspeakable joy of seeing many brought to the Saviour. Truly, it was a scene we do not often see; for one Sunday, in the large Town Hall, men and women were smitten down under the power of the Word, backsliders reclaimed and brought back to the deserted fold. In this town many of my little books were put into the hands of those who had lived "without God and without hope in the world," and I have pleasure in saying they have not been read in vain.* In addition to this, one young woman stopped me going from the Hall, and said: "Thank God for sending you here. My mother had a bad daughter last week; she has a good one this." Another young woman said: "As I heard you speaking on Sunday night the words came home to my heart—'Are we blind also?' I went home and found Christ at my bedside. Thanks be unto God and the Lamb! 'for his mercy endureth for ever.'"

The Lord then sent me to a place called Swinton, among the colliers. I had been in the pit of sin, and I had a word for my brother colliers. The village was placarded, and on the Sunday night the place was so full many had to go back. At the close, many confessed they had found the Lord. During the week the village was well canvassed by our dear brother, Mr. Gerrard, and myself. We had some happy meetings. Many came to Jesus, like Mary, and went home rejoicing. We had an experience meeting at the close of my stay there; and one of the new converts, a young man about twenty-four, said, when he got up to speak, "Bless the Lord for what he has done for me! I was asked by a shopmate to come and hear Harry preach at the

* The above account appeared in *The Christian.*

Primitive Chapel. I said, 'What Harry?' 'Come and see,' said my mate. I told him my wife could preach enough to me—too much. I wanted none of Harry's preaching. But he begged of me to come. I heard Harry, and Harry persuaded me to come again. I came again. At work next day I wished it was night, to get to hear Harry again. Night came, and, through Harry, Christ found me out—a poor sinner." "God bless Harry!" he cried. Both him and his wife were made happy. "Blessed be the name of the Lord!"

I was then led to Stockport, where, also, my labours proved a blessing; and as I have often heard objections raised by those who do not agree with putting bills out to attract the wicked, let me here ask, "If the devil had clothed me, in a convict prison, with a Government suit marked all over with 'City Prison,' or 'Convict Prison,' for fear I should make my escape, shall I shrink from putting 'Converted Convict' on a bill for Jesus, to show the world what God has done for me?" Oh, no, reader, "for the children of this world are in their generation wiser than the children of light;" and ever since God converted my soul I have been willing to be a "door-keeper," a "hewer of wood or drawer of water;" "yea, all things to all men, that I may win some." The bill that was put out in this town was: "Come and hear H. Holloway, the converted convict, from Gibraltar." Let us see how God used this bill at first. During these services there might have been seen a poor woman standing at the canal side, just about to put an end to her life by drowning herself, when suddenly her eye caught the bill above-mentioned. "What!" said she, the Lord saved a convict! Surely He can save a poor outcast like me." While I was preaching this poor woman might be seen coming in at the door of the chapel, when she burst into tears, and said, "Will God save me?" "Oh, yes," I said, "my dear woman, Christ came to seek and to save the lost." Christ did save her soul. She told us how she was nearly lost. When her eye caught the bill she said, "I'll go and hear him." My dear reader, I had the unspeakable joy of seeing that poor unfortunate nicely lodged in a comfortable home in Manchester before I slept that night.

Reader, what drew her attention first? The bill. Then Christ saved her. May I ask you if ever the Cross and Jesus upon it ever had a charm for you? Are you destroying yourself in sin like the above? Will you come to Jesus? There is life for a look; and if you will only raise your wishful eye and take your sinful heart to Jesus you shall find happiness, like the star upon the brow of night; and, while gazing upon the Crucified One, from His precious blood your faith shall fetch in pardon for all your sin; and, like the writer of this book, "rejoice with joy unspeakable and full of glory." This dear woman was one out of many to whom the Saviour said, "Go in peace and sin no more."

Here I received a letter to go to Sydenham, near London, from a lady well known in that locality, who had been savingly converted to God, and, hearing of my labours in the Lancashire districts, sent for me. I went, but here I had a hard struggle with Satan and his satanic powers. I had been preaching about a week, night after night, in the Gospel Hall, formerly a singing saloon, with much blessing, when it was proposed that I should preach outside in the open air. We went out one Sunday afternoon, the weather being fine; it was about three o'clock, just as the men were being turned out of the public-house by the publican. It afforded me much pleasure to see the working men, some of whom were worse for liquor, flock round to hear the Gospel. I gave out the little hymn—

Strike the harps of heaven, there is joy to-day
For a soul returning from the wild
See the Father meets him out upon the way,
Welcoming his weary wandering child, &c.

We had scarcely got through the second verse when the

landlord of the hotel or public-house came rushing at me like a lion. " I'll not have that preaching here," cried he. " Beg pardon," said I, " who are you, sir ? " " Who am I ? I'll let you see who I am. I am the landlord of that public-house. I'll not have you preaching here." " I am very sorry to offend you," I said. " I thought I should give no offence here. Our service should have commenced at half-past two, but we thought we would not begin till you closed your house at three; then you would see we did not offer any opposition against your trade. But may I ask you a question?" said I. " Is this your ground ? " " No," said he, " but I'll not have you here." " Well," said I, " 'The earth is the Lord's and the fulness thereof,' and I shall not move from my Master's ground." " I'll fetch a policeman," he said, and away he went and brought him. The policeman came to me and said, " You will have to go away from here, my man." Dear reader, this nearly broke my heart, to think I must go off when I was on a waste ground obstructing no thoroughfare whatever. By this time a large crowd had gathered round, and the publican stood sneering at the corner of his house with a large cigar in his mouth, to think how grand he'd done it to fetch the policeman. But, praise the Lord! Harry was one of those sort of champions for Christ that did not fear persecution. I said to the policeman, " Look here, sir, I am willing to obey you, but if I move from here on this good Sabbath afternoon, through the influence of that publican, the Gospel will not have the least weight about here." Then I addressed the policeman in the following words : " Sir, will you please to let me stop and preach here to these working men and women ? If I am breaking the law, take my name—I will appear to all; if not, let me preach. Do you know who I am ? " I said. " I have come 200 miles to deliver my message for God ; and, more than that, I have been a man whom the strong hand of the law has gripped and fastened to the whipping-post—not for preaching, but for dishonesty

D

and creating disturbances when in a state of intoxication. Mr. Policeman, when I used to get drunk and make a noise in the streets, you gentlemen would not let me alone; and now that Christ, my Saviour, has reached my wicked heart and made me a new creature, and I want to benefit my fellow-man, won't you let me alone now?" I said, " The police of Manchester would scorn the action to attempt to move me for preaching Christ." I need only say this had such an influence on all around that the policeman stood by and listened attentively to the Gospel. The repentant tear was seen to fall as I told the story of the Cross and what God had done for me. Here applause arose from the listeners—"God bless you, lad!" When I got off the chair on which I stood I got a hearty shake of the hand from many who, I have reason to believe, were much blessed. At night the hall was crowded, many of whom would have been in the public-house had they not have heard the Gospel in the streets. In this place I remained for one month, night after night, uplifting the standard of the Cross. Many homes that were wretched and miserable became, like Martha and Mary's at Bethany, happy, because Jesus was there. To God be all the glory !

I now left Sydenham for Manchester, and for a number of months preached the Gospel in fairs, wakes, halls, and chapels of different denominations with much blessing. All the while I felt that God was with me. The reason I knew that God honoured the open-air work so much was this—and it may be of use to those who would like to do something for their Master—no matter wherever I went to preach I used to get the working men on my side. Why was this? Because God has kept me in the manger of humility. Thank God, I have never let the hedge grow too high but that I would always jump into a hole and shake hands with a navvy or a poor drunkard in the gutter. My Master took the blind by the hand, and that teaches me a lesson to try and lead those who are blind in sin into the glorious sunshine of the people of God.

It was the custom always to pay toll in markets or fairs. To stand up and get a crowd round you to hear the Gospel a shilling was the fee generally, and as sure as I paid it some one in the congregation was sure to return it back to me. Praise the Lord! One time I was preaching in a public market, when I said to the people, "I am very tired and thirsty, but I am not going into yonder public-house to get a drink. I have been in there too often." "Stay a minute," cried a dear woman in the crowd, "I'll fetch thee something to eat and drink too." And in ten minutes this good woman returned with a jug of nice tea, with milk in it, along with a plate of ham sandwiches. Glory be to God! The Lord caused the ravens to feed Elijah, and now He was feeding me; and so will it be with all who go out fulfilling the Master's words, "Go ye into all the world, and preach the gospel to every creature." I have seen the poor drunkard, harlot, and thief listening till the tears have rolled down their cheeks; and from such meetings as these I have had the joy of removing many of our daughters of shame into a place of comfort and happiness.

These meetings led to an engagement with Mr. A. Alsop, who for years had been labouring among the most wretched and degraded population in the city of Manchester. My heart yearned to get at them. By the assistance of kind friends Brother Alsop had managed to build a church, which he named the Working Men's Church. Here I was engaged for some time to hold special services; and never, as long as I live, shall I forget the great work that God wrought out for the fallen there. The first day of the mission, Mr. Alsop and I went to visit the homes of the poor and sinful. While conversing from house to house, and inviting to the church, many were led to abandon their evil course of life and flee to Christ, who will turn none away. The first night of our mission the place was crowded, and precious souls found Jesus. Among them was one returned convict, four unfortunates, who were removed into a happy home, and, strange to say, one old woman found Christ that I used to torment to death nearly when I was a bad lad. She used to run after me with a stick, and swear she would break my back; but, praise the Lord! while I was preaching the Gospel the Lord broke her hard heart, and healed it again with Gilead's balm. Hallelujah! The work became so much noised abroad in every house I was obliged to send back word declining some engagements, because the Lord was working so powerfully amongst us. Many poor fallen sisters were brought to Christ, taken off the streets, and got good situations, some of whom, to-day, are an honour to their country and the society to which they belong. It, perhaps, would be wise of me to name one case of great interest, showing the goodness of God to take the very dregs of a sinful life and build it up into a temple of holiness and purity. One night as I was preaching from the "Prodigal," I said : "My dear brothers and sisters, I am before many, to-night, who knew me when I was like themselves—(the reader will observe it was to this very Lombard Street, where I was now preaching, that I first came when I began my career of crime, taking up my abode in a lodging-house, not being long there before I was lodged in prison)—and if you look upon the past of your lives, can you not remember when your dear mothers took you upon their knees, and there taught you that little prayer—

Gentle Jesus meek and mild,
Look upon a little child ?

Can you forget those days ? Is not the memory of them fresh in your heart, to-night, though you are blasted with sin, feeding upon the husks—far from Zion, far from God, and without hope in the world ? I, like some of you, resolved to leave my home, though I was blessed with a praying mother who taught me to love Christ ; but, like the Prodigal in the chapter we are speaking about, I wandered into a far country, almost lost my soul, broke my poor mother's heart, and brought her grey hairs down with sorrow to the grave. But, thanks be unto God ! the magnetic power of that mother's prayer comforted me whilst under penal servitude for seven years, and sometimes I even thought I heard my mother crying outside the prison, 'O Harry, give thy heart to God, and all will yet be well.' " Reader, if you had been there that night you would have seen the poor Magdalene weeping at the feet of Jesus, like the poor woman did in Simon's house. "Ah, my dear friends," I said, "you may be poor and sinful. Come to Jesus. He will save just now." Here I stopped preaching, the whole congregation wept ; and to have seen the sorrow depicted in the faces of some that had not been washed for days, with their eyes suffused with tears, told a tale of no light suffering. One poor woman who was wrought upon by the Holy Spirit, and induced to give herself to Jesus, told me the following sad story of her life. She, too, like myself, had been blessed with a praying mother, but, like many more, had hated counsel and despised reproof. She left home and went to service in Liverpool. Here, for a time, she was very comfortable in a situation as servant, but, thinking she would like to see some friends in Manchester, she came here unfortunately, got entangled with some man, who led her astray, induced her to leave her place, and, alas, like many more, left her blasted with sin as a daughter of shame. Her first inducement was this : she was met by a female in the street when inquiring her way in Manchester, and took by the person alluded to a lodging-house ; here she was induced to lend her clothes to one of the inmates in the house by being deceived in the statement made by the person who borrowed them saying she wanted to get a situation. The woman, simple enough, lent them, but she never had them returned ; and, after pawning and selling the rest, she was, she said, "as you see me at this present moment." This was, reader, with just an old dress to cover her naked body.   But Christ took her in, and through the influence of Mr. Alsop she was sent to a home for the fallen.   A week after her manners and abilities got her a good situation.   Let us say, to God be all the glory for lifting her out of the pit of sin into the path of safety and peace.   The Lord hath a mighty arm, stretched out wide, returning sinners to receive.   This night was a scene I shall never forget.   The work went on night after night.   It was a precious soul-saving time. Such an influence had God wrought upon some who had left their haunts of vice and sin that many, more hardened than others, as I went in and out of the lodgings, accompanied by Brother Alsop, would shout to me: "Don't you speak to my 'bloke'" (meaning fancy-man, spoony-man, or in some cases it might be the real husband). The reason of this was, God was so good, was so wonderfully using me, that many who came in contact with the Word were caught in the Gospel net, and made happy in Jesus.   Praise the Lord!   It was thought advisable to visit a neighbourhood about a mile from the church.   In this neighbourhood there were from forty to fifty thieves and poor fallen women living in some of the houses.   Charles Goodier, of Manchester (well known as a poor sinner saved), accompanied by Mr. Alsop, went to visit the above, and invited the people to come and hear Holloway preach the Gospel.   In these dens we persuaded no less than six poor unfortuates to at once leave their present course of living.   A cab was sent for, and we had the joy of seeing them removed to the home in Coupland Street, Manchester.   Some of these girls had men living with them, but they were as tired of them as they were of sin.   At night, as I was going into the church to preach, I was stopped by a woman, who told me the following: She had overheard no less than nine of these men who lived in these dens of infamy concocting together to seize me in the streets and illuse me for taking away their women.   I escaped their hands like Paul did, and when I began to preach at night they were all in the church.

I made no personal remarks. I knew the story of David and the giant, and I well knew that Jesus told his disciples, "Behold, I send you forth as lambs among wolves," and, having been a champion for Satan, I was not frightened to meet a Goliath in sin, for my God has said, "My word shall not return unto me void." My text that night was John iv., 4, "He must needs go through Samaria." I began to talk of that living water which Christ had given me and the poor woman at the well. "Oh, yes, my friends," I said, "the great love of Jesus can penetrate the darkest corners of the human heart, and light up a pathway there and lead you on to heaven. There may be some here who are rough and vile, poor and sinful, outcasts from society, known by nobody scarcely but the magistrates, police, and prison authorities; but Christ can save you like he did me and this poor woman of whom I speak. God grant that your cry may be heard to-night in the following." Here I sang—

### AWAKENED SINNER.

What shall I do to be saved?
Weeping and trembling with fear!
Roused by conviction I wake,
Sinai's loud thunder I hear.
Now, on the brink of despair,
Death and destruction I see:
What shall I do to be saved?
Is there redemption for me?

CHORUS:
What shall I do, what shall I do,
What shall I do to be saved?

I have rejected, with scorn,
Blessings I might have received;
Often the Spirit of grace
Wounded, insulted, and grieved;
Broken the law of my God,
Nailed him again to the tree:
Can I forgiveness implore?
Is there salvation for me?
What shall I do, &c.

I to my Father will go:
Now, like the prodigal son,
Down at his feet I will fall,
Tell him the wrong I have done;
There, if I perish, I'll pray;
This my petition shall be—
Lord, I repent and believe;
Jesus, have mercy on me.
This will I do, &c.

A deep feeling prevailed throughout the place. During prayer two of these characters were powerfully wrought upon by the Holy Ghost. One of them was savingly brought to Jesus, and is now doing well; while the other went back into sin, and is now under penal servitude for seven years. Since he has been in prison he has seen the folly of not taking the advice from friends who wished him well. May God save his soul! Reader, art thou leading such a life as this? If so, the "way of transgressors is hard." "Be sure your sin will find you out." If you go undetected all your life there will come a time when the eternal Judge will sit before you to pass the sentence; and let me tell you, if you do not repent and return to God this side the grave it will be sure to be "guilty." Then you will say, "What a fool I have been to have hated instruction and despised reproof. Now God is laughing at my calamity; he is mocking now my fear has come." This need not be, my friend and brother. God can save you like he did me. I pray him to open your eyes before you read another line. Be resolved to come to Christ, and, though you are branded with sin, Jesus will receive you and give to you the kiss, the robe, and the ring, and make you happy in his forgiving love.

There was one thing in connection with these services that was the sole means of our success, that was our daily prayer meetings. I have seen as many as one hundred people there from the mills and shops around, who would come in after dinner if it was only to offer their prayer and go off to work again. Many a precious soul have we had in the daily prayer meetings. The following will give the reader an insight into God's mercy if he should not know it. One day as we were at prayer an object of pity entered the church, with neither shoes nor stockings on, and, what is more, he had no shirt on. His knees smote together with the cold, for the keen winds of March were blowing. We had a large fire in the place; I took him up to it, and while he was warming himself he said, "How kind you are to me! I have not seen a fire for a long time." We knelt together in prayer; the big tears rolled down his cheeks. This was truly a scene of sorrow. After prayer, I put a few questions to him, and begged of him to answer them in truth, seeing that he looked to me as if he had just come out of prison. l said, "May I ask you have you not been in prison lately?" The man replied: "Well, if I must tell the truth, I have just come out of prison this morning; I belong to London; I am a stranger here; I have been on the bridge of the canal to throw myself in, and oh, what a mercy that God has stopped me!" I knew that the poor man must be hungry, so I took him at once to a cook-shop, gave him his dinner, went back to the church (with Mr. A. Alsop, the superintendent of the church), took him and stripped him, bought him new clogs, stockings, clothes, &c., and to-day he is a miracle of grace and an honour to the city of Manchester.

After reading the above, will anybody deny the mercy of God? He doth take the dregs off a man's life in his mercy, and we are led to say in this case, as well as myself, "Is not this a brand plucked out of the fire?" Read the third chapter of Zechariah. There you will see a parallel case to the above. "God hath a mighty arm; he can save and none can hinder." So widely was the Gospel preached around this modern Babylon, that some said, like they did of Paul, &c., "These men that have turned the world upside down have come hither also." It was nothing new for a poor girl that had brought disgrace upon herself and parents to decide at once to give up her evil course, and lead an honest and pure life, and, like the woman of Samaria, go into the city to say, "Come, see a man that told me all things that ever I did." They are to be found—some of whom were brought to Christ during these services—on a Saturday night especially, amidst the revelry of sin, distributing tracts and speaking a word for Jesus to poor sinners.

I was forced to leave Lombard Street to go elsewhere. The next place I went to was a mission in Ordsall Lane, Salford. Here we had a good time, although we did not see a Pentecostal shower of blessing; yet the Master has said—"In the morning sow thy seed, and in the evening withhold not thine hand; for thou knowest not what shall prosper, either this or that, or whether they both shall be alike good." Truly the Lord was with us, and several found Jesus.

I remained here a week. On Saturday I left to take up a few short engagements in and round Manchester. Some of the readers of the *Christian* will remember seeing an account of the Mission Hall floor giving way, and precipitating 150 people, young and old, into a coalyard below. This happened the very week after I had been preaching, while the dear brethren were met for a tea party. Among the injured ones was a dear brother, Mr. Dougal, who had taken an active part in the service the week before. He received a compound fracture, and was taken to the Dispensary with other sufferers. Here a scene occurred which deserves notice, to show the reader how a dying Christian can rejoice in suffering and in death. As his case was the worst of all that were injured, the doctor came to dress his wounds first, when he turned to him and asked, "Why do you dress my wounds first?" "Oh, my man," said the doctor, "you are hurt the worst." "Ah, that may be; but I want you to dress them first." "Why?" asked the doctor. "Oh," said he, "I am prepared to die; they are not. Do dress them first, will you?" Here this dying man of God, though full of pain, broke out and sung in that hospital—

I have a beautiful land on high, &c.

He still continued to repeat—

In that beautiful land I'll be
From pain and from sin set free;
My Jesus is there, he's gone to prepare
A place in that land for me.

After lingering a short time he died, and went to be with Jesus, which is far better. Oh, reader, art thou prepared to die? Remember, ere long your eyes that gaze upon these pages will become dim, and, if not ready, what will you do in the hour of death? Faithful are the wounds of a friend. But there is another that was wounded for your transgressions and bruised for your iniquities, and though you have gone astray like a lost sheep the Lord hath laid on him (Jesus) the iniquities of us all. And though, reader, you may be the worst sinner in the world, Christ comes to you, like as the doctor came to this poor man, first. Christ comes to thee to bind up thy sinful heart, and heal it with the balm of Gilead. "Wilt thou be made whole?" Let the goodness of God lead you to repentance, and whilst you are looking at Jesus by faith on the Cross, you shall find salvation through the precious blood of the Lamb; but if you put it off, "how shall you escape if you neglect so great a salvation?"

After labouring for a short time in my own town, Manchester and suburbs, one night, as I entered the hall where I was preaching, I was accosted by about ten men, who said to me, "What's going to be up there to-night?" I said, "'Come and see.' There is a man who was formerly a prize-fighter in the devil's service going to fight a battle with Satan." "Are you the man?" said one. "Yes," I said. With this, one of them said, "I'll fight you for five pounds." "Well, my good friend," I said, "one day I would have taken the challenge in a moment. I once fought for money, and to please other people, but to-day I am fighting for Christ—fighting for a crown that's laid up in heaven for me." "Then you won't fight me?" cried one. I said, "Don't run it on to me, or take me out winding, for I used to understand a little about the P.R. But I must go in to fight here," I said. "If you will come into that hall I will fight the whole ten of you with this book," drawing out of my pocket my Bible. They came in, and listened with great attention, as I spoke on fighting men and their gains and losses. It was all losses, no gains—loss of character, and, in the end, loss of soul for ever. What I said made a deep impression, accompanied by the Holy Spirit of God. At the close I had the unspeakable joy of seeing three out of the ten brought to Christ. One of them was scoffing in the prayer meeting, and I went to him, and asked him did his wife send him there to mock God. "I've got no wife," he said. "Well, my friend," I said, "did your dear mother send you here?" "Ah," said the man, "if mother had been alive I should not be what I am to-day." Tears began to flow down his cheeks. His companions asked him was he going to turn soft. "Turn soft," he said; "If this is turning soft, what Holloway has got it makes him happy; and by God's help I'll have it before I leave this hall to-night, and praise God with others." He decided for Christ, left his companions, and to-day he is a happy man.

"My word shall not return unto me void. . . . Instead of the thorn shall come up the fir tree, and instead of the brier shall come up the myrtle tree; and it shall be to the Lord for a name, for an everlasting sign that shall not be cut off." (Isaiah lv., 11, 13.)

At the same hall there was a poor young woman, twenty years of age, in a most wretched condition, brought to Jesus. She was clothed, fed, and a situation got for her, and she like many more received the truth. "Fear thou not, for I am with thee; be not dismayed for I am thy God: I will never leave thee nor forsake thee."

After this, my mind was led to go to London, to preach at the Edinburgh Castle, Limehouse; and, after staying there a fortnight, and seeing a few interesting cases of conversion, I left to go to Mr. Lewis's Mission Hall, Spitalfields, Brick Lane, E.C. In connection with these services we met for prayer every day from three to four o'clock. Mr. Lewis had bills printed and well circulated by members of the place, and on my first night of being there large numbers thronged to hear the word of life.

We went out into the open air, down the streets of some of the darkest spots in the east of London, visiting lodging-houses, giving invitations to some of the poor and degraded of that locality. It was a season of joy to my soul to see the poor wanderers of all classes enter the meetings—young girls, some not more than fourteen years of age, who had been led astray by evil men, thrown on the streets, and left to the mercy of the world. One night—I shall never forget the scene that exhibited itself; it was the sight of sin-sick souls—when I entered the hall I intended, by the help of God, to speak a few words from Amos iv., 12; but when I looked round upon the congregation, some of whom seemed heart-broken before the service commenced, I was led to put this text away for the night and take another—Proverbs xxiii., 29-32. I began by saying, " Looking round upon this congregation, I see before me many in whose face is the painful index of no light suffering. Well might the Scripture say, ' Who hath woe. Who hath sorrow?' Have not some of you? We need not go out of this room to learn that." " No, my lad," cried a woman in the meeting, " I have enough of sorrow through it." " Yes," said I. " What is it that will take the bloom from your cheek and the brightness from your eye? Drink. Was any of you ever in a convict prison? I hope not; but, if so, did you ever notice the convicts in chains as they paced up and down in their cells, or at work, or whenever they moved, each stride they took seemed to cry out, by the chains, "Drink! Drink! Drink!" You shall go to any prison in the world, and visit each prisoner separately, ask him or her the cause of their being there, and ninety-nine cases out of every hundred will attribute the cause to drink. Is it not true, my dear friends? Experience is a good teacher, and no man can rob another of it. If any man can say to the contrary to what I state I should like to hear him." I then told a few cases that had come under my notice. The following was one: I was in a village about four miles from Manchester, preaching the Gospel in a small Primitive Chapel. As I was going round, giving some small hand-bills out, I came across a poor ragged-looking woman, who was weeping bitterly. I asked the cause of her grief. She replied 'I cannot help weeping. I and my children are clothed in rags, and my husband takes nearly all his money to the public-house. But a few minutes ago I went to the back door to draw some water, when the landlord's wife came out of the house where my husband spends all his money nearly. She said to me, when she saw my ragged dress, 'Are you not ashamed to come out in a dress like that?' The tears began to flow down my cheeks as I said to her, 'It is well to be you, to have a silk dress on, out of the poor working men's wages; and I can tell you, Mrs. Publican, if my husband would keep outside your house I could dress as well as you."

Reader, are you a working-man? If so, I beg of you not to let these high priests of unrighteousness have another penny of your hard-earnings. Do not be attracted by the glaring gaslight in their vaults, but let your attention be at home with your sons there. Their large taproom fires may charm you, but you can have one at home if you will keep your money. "He lieth in wait secretly, as a lion in his den: he lieth in wait to catch the poor: he doth catch the poor when he draweth him into his net." Suppose I were going down one of the streets in London, and a mad dog ran from somewhere and bit me, and, coming along the street, I met you about to go down past the dog. Would it not be unkind on my part if I did not warn you of the danger? So, my friend, I have been bitten by the demon Drink; I have felt its curse. It is able to fell the strongest man, and, as one who has been taught in a dear school, I warn you against this deadly poison. Some people call it mild—I call it very bitter. Others call it pale—yes, true, it has made many poor children pale, many a poor wife pale. It took the bloom from my cheeks; it was the means of taking me into the depths of sin I went into; and, but for the grace of God, I might have been in hell, lost for ever. Oh, working man, if such you are, let me ask you whose fault will it be if you don't get to heaven? I would not have written this book if it were not to try and do you good. "What shall it profit a man if he gain the world and lose his own soul?" This is a question which I hope you will consider before you sleep to-night. You may say, if you had been as wicked as I have been, it would be time to repent and turn to God. Let me tell you, dear reader, you have a soul that will live for ever, either in a state of happiness and bliss, or misery and despair. Eternity, how long art thou? For ever! Where shall I spend it? Your soul has been purchased at a dear rate. It cost the blood of Christ to redeem man; and as long as you keep back from God what has been bought by the death of Jesus, you are a thief and a robber. Therefore I entreat you to make no more delay, but go to Christ: He has saved me—He will save you.

Here I made an appeal to those who had left their homes, and wandered, like the Prodigal Son, into a far country. Though the door of their parental home was closed against them, the door of mercy was not. I told them of a poor girl who had been led astray by a bad young man. She was an honest girl, had a praying father and mother; but accompanied a young man on an excursion trip. He seemed to be alone; but, like many more, he had his bosom friend with him. That friend was the demon Drink, in the shape of a black bottle of rum. She was asked to drink time after time on the way. She did so. Alas! she fell: was ruined, blasted with sin, and at last found herself on the streets as a daughter of shame, in a far country, without friends or home. There she was going to put an end to herself, but something said, "Ellen, go home to thy mother; she is dying of a broken heart." She turned round instead of destroying herself, and burst into tears. When some one inquired the cause of her grief, she told them. A good gentleman in the company said, " I will put you into a cab, and send you to the station to your mother's home." " No, no," she cried, " I have left home and brought this sorrow upon myself and my dear mother, who I know is breaking her heart for me. I'll go home, but I will foot it all the way back, weary as I am." She did go home ; the door had never been closed against her ; her mother had never ceased to pray for her all the time she had been away. She was received back with joy, and as soon as she entered the house, mother and daughter were locked in each other's arms.

" Poor wanderers here to-night, are you not like this young woman ? Have you not left your home, and wandered into the beggarly elements of the world ? What have you gained by it all ? Go back home, friends, if you have one. Remember, you are breaking your parents' hearts, who are sorrowing on your account. But, above all, come home to Christ to-night. ' I am the way, the truth, and the life.' ' I am the door ; by Me if any man (and when it says man it means woman too) enters in, he shall be saved, and go in and out, and shall find pasture.' Come home, poor drunkard, to Jesus. Come to Jesus, fallen sister, and as you have to-night heard of the riches of the new Jerusalem, and how to attain them by Christ ; believe the report, turn your back upon sin and give your heart to God. God grant I may meet you in the home of eternal repose."

I had been to Mr. Scott, at the office of *The Christian*, and told him where I was preaching, and said it was no use me staying there if there was no place to remove the poor fallen women to, when they were sincere and willing to abandon their evil course. He gave me a letter to go to Mr. Thomas, 200, Euston Road. I told him there were a number of poor girls desirous of leaving the path of sin. This kind gentleman told me to bring four to him. I may say that at the close of the address above referred to, with the assistance of the male and female missionaries kept by Mr. Lewis, we were dealing with no less than fifteen poor outcasts, thieves and fallen women. They were weeping on one another's necks bitterly. Some found Jesus, went home at once, while others who had no home resolved to go into the homes provided for them. Next day I had the happiness to take four to Mr. Thomas, and he received them, in addition to one whom her mother brought herself; she had not fallen, but her friends were afraid she would. I saw her into the home. Our dear brother Lewis had gone to the country to recruit his health a little, having for many years toiled hard against Satan in that locality. It rejoiced his heart to hear the good news. I will just draw the attention of the reader, if a female. Dear friend, if you were just to go and visit the slums and alleys of this neighbourhood you would, I am sure, never enter a public-house again. As it is, after reading what drink has done for me and thousands besides, never darken the door of a public-house. Again, one of the above girls told one of her own sex that at thirteen years of age she was decoyed away from home by a man much older than herself, drugged, and ruined by him. Oh, young woman, do come to Jesus. Do not say you are too good to fall. I was once an honest lad; learned to sing of Jesus at my mother's knee; heard of Christ in the Sunday School. Bad company was the first step, and from one thing to another I found myself in a convict cell. Let me ask you, as one of God's children, not to keep company with evil young men. Does not reason tell you if the men with whom you have fellowship do not love God they cannot love you? You will have sorrow while you are single; if married you will have sorrow to the very dregs. Take a pattern by the following extract from one of Mr. W. Birch's sermons: "A young woman who used to get her living by dressmaking (it was before sewing machines

E

were in common use) found it was very hard to make both ends meet. But she loved Christ, who had promised to take care of her. One day as she was out in the street she was followed by a man of fashion. She repelled him, but he followed her to her home. She told him to be gone. Next day she received a letter. On breaking the seal she found a Bank of England note, with th following: 'My dear ——, With the enclosed buy suitable clothes for yourself, and meet me at Victoria Station at ——, and I will take you to the Isle of Man.' As soon as she read this tears rolled down her cheeks. But she looked up to God and said, 'Death rather than sin.'" Oh, reader! will you imitate this noble act if ever you should be tempted? Remember, "Many are the afflictions of the righteous; but the Lord delivereth them out of them all." Look to Jesus, my dear readers! Beware of the first step; and when tempted to forsake your God and to give up the contest listen to the voice which says, "Look up, 'tis better on before." Reader, are you yet in sin? "Be sure your sin will find you out." If it does not now it will at the Judgment Day. Are you young? Read Eccles. xii.; and may God, for Christ's sake, save your soul.

I left this mission and went and held a few open-air meetings in different places, with many blessings from on high. After this I returned to Manchester to fulfil a few short engagements. Space will not allow me to dwell on the success that God wrought out through His humble servant; but let me here say that in some of the villages near Manchester the light of the glorious Gospel has so won its way, by God's blessing, that it is burning yet in many hearts who are on their way to heaven. I laboured at Whitworth, near Rochdale, with much blessing; and was led by the Lord to Hazel Grove, near Stockport, where I was told the people were so hard that nothing would move them. The Saturday before I preached I went through the village with my bell, inviting the people to come, and on the following day (Sunday) the place was so full there was no sitting down. My little book, called " A Voice from the Convict Cell," was read with great delight, for I received a letter from a brother, saying that it had made a lasting impression upon many : and by the power of the Holy Spirit I hope they were saved. I only stayed here a few days, but, thank God, with much blessing ; for I heard that after I left the village a revival broke out—a thorough working of God broke out. God sent me, I suppose, to turn up the fallow ground, sow the seed, and then He sent the reapers. Praise the Lord.

I was led by the Spirit of God to take Hulme Town Hall, in Manchester, for Sunday services, twice each day. I always felt a burning desire to preach in that hall, for a good reason, which I will name. Before this spacious building was erected it was a waste ground, where all sorts of revelry and sin were carried on ; but on Sundays numbers used to assemble to preach the Gospel. I used to go there to scoff at them when I was a bad man ; and on one occasion I remember fighting with a policeman on the very ground that the Town Hall now stands. This was the reason I wanted God to use me on the same ground as the devil had. I laid the case before the Lord. He said " Go." I took it for a few weeks. On the Sunday I commenced Mr. Thomas Wright, prison philanthropist, opened the services. The place was full in the afternoon. Mr. Wright said he was glad to meet Brother Holloway on occasions like the present, for he heard he was brought to Christ, but he had never seen him since he visited him in prison. He said much more ; earnestly entreating the young to give themselves to God now. He said how many he had seen have the rope put round their necks on the scaffold, and many of them could say if they had listened to the voice of their parents, and teachers, and friends, and kept from drink and bad company, they would never have been brought to a death like that.

This was a great time. A deep feeling prevailed throughout the service, and it was brought to a close. In the evening it was full again. I preached from the words of our Saviour, " What think ye of Christ ?" At the close we held a prayer-meeting. Many found the Lord, and went home rejoicing in Jesus. With the assistance of a few friends, the expense being great, I was able to go on for some time. One Sunday, above all others, after I had given an address from the words, " Wilt thou be made whole ?" the people seemed to flock out as if they had come through curiosity—just as if they had heard an idle tale. I don't know how it was that night, but I felt very unhappy, especially when I saw all the people going out. I went into one corner of the room, and spoke to my Master, Jesus, and said, " Lord, wilt Thou not give me souls for this night's labour ?" I then gave out the hymn,

Depth of mercy can there be, &c.,

when the people began to come back. After prayer, while going round from one to another, asking them, " What think ye of Christ ?" I observed a man full length by himself on the seat, his face buried in his hands. I said to him, " Friend, have you got a load in that heart of yours ?" " A load ! Ah, yes, I have—a load that I will get rid of to-night." " Where are you going to—home ?" I asked. With this the man rose up and said, " I once ran well, but, in an evil hour, I have gone back into the wilderness of sin. I am wretched." He then walked up to the platform, fell down on his knees, and prayed for God to restore unto him the joy of His salvation, and uphold him with His free Spirit. This night was a season of joy to me to see one and another come forward and give themselves to Jesus. Surely, the kingdom of heaven was suffering violence, and the violent taking it by force. One young woman, about twenty-one years of age, rushed from her seat, fell down on her knees, and cried for mercy. It was a touching scene. No sooner had God pardoned her, than her dear mother, who was in the hall, came and fell down beside her daughter, praying, "Glory! glory! glory! I have been looking and waiting for this for years." And, turning to me, she said, "God bless you, Mr. Holloway, for ever coming to this hall to bring my child to Christ." "Jesus did it all my friend," I said. That night precious souls found Jesus, and went down to their homes happy.

I stayed here a few weeks, preaching twice each Sunday, and then I left for the city of London once more. The first appointment I had to take was at Golden Lane Mission Hall, under the superintendence of Mr. Orsman, who for many years has been labouring there amongst the poor of that locality. Here I was not ashamed of Jesus. Before I began to preach I went out with my Gospel-bell down the slums that surround that neighbourhood. Something occurred here which I had never met with before. I think the name of the street was Whitecross, or Whitehorse Street. I was ringing my bell, when I was completly surrounded by a mob of costers, &c. As I passed down the streets, which were thronged with stalls, &c., the butchers cried out, "Give us a ring, gov'nor." Well, I thought I would not be unkind to them, so I rung my bell, got a crowd round, advertised the meat for sale, then told them to come to Golden Lane Mission, and there they would get a feast for nothing. Many thronged to hear the Word of Life night after night. One night I stood at the corner of the lane, inviting the people in. I was just going into the hall, when some person sent a large potato at me. It struck me right in the ear, but it was only like water on a duck's back, it rolled off; or, like the viper that fastened on St. Paul's hand, I shook it off. I had often been knocked down with a policeman's staff when serving the devil, so I was not to be daunted for my Master, Like Paul, I said, "None of these things move me, for I bear in my body the marks of the Lord Jesus Christ." With much blessing I laboured here a week, and then removed to King Street Hall, Longacre, W., under the superintendence of Mr. G. Hatton. It was the mission week in February; and, thank God, it was a mission of mercy to many poor sinners. The members of this place, along with their faithful leader, had been looking for a long time for the Lord to make bear His arm in the salvation of precious and immortal souls. Time after time they had met for prayer for wicked St. Giles's. God heard their prayer and saved many precious souls. Truly, it was a time of refreshing from the presence of the Lord. From St. Giles's Christian Mission, a correspondent wrote to *The Christian* :—

"Join with us in praise for what our eyes have seen of God's work during the last few days! Truly it has been a time of refreshing from the presence of the Lord. Mr. H. Holloway, from Manchester, has been preaching the Gospel to the masses during the mission week. The meetings were commenced outdoors on Sunday morning in the Seven Dials, followed by a gathering of believers in the hall. Special prayer for the mighty power of the Spirit to accompany all Gospel testimony in London during the week, interspersed with short addresses by the Hon. Thomas Pelham, and Messrs. Clarke and Groves. This was a blessed season, and deep feeling was manifest. In the evening the hall was thronged with an audience characteristic of St. Giles's. After Mr. Holloway's address large numbers made their way to the inquiry-rooms, seeking Jesus; and not a few obtained peace and joy in believing. Every night since the building has been packed in every nook and corner, and many scores of anxious inquirers it has been our joy to direct to the Lamb of God. The meetings are still continued, and seem to increase in interest each night."

If I were to cite the different cases of conversion that came under my notice at this mission I could fill a book. There was one beautiful feature in connection with these services that was the great lever to awake dead souls to a

living Christ—that was constant and untiring prayer with
the Master. Day after day we met at noonday, and
there was realised the presence of Jesus not only to our
own souls, but we had the unspeakable joy of seeing more
than one or two convinced and converted in these daily
prayer meetings. The following will testify for itself
that God was with us, and we well know "if God be for us
who can be against." "If the work be of God ye cannot
overthrow ; if it be of men it will come to naught." One
day, as we were at prayer, there came in a young man,
whose outward appearance told a tale for itself—that
there was something more than mere distress. He looked
as if he had seen better days. During the whole of the
prayer there was a struggle going on between the lion of
hell and the "Lion of the tribe of Judah." In short, the
man, who was deeply convinced of sin, after a long struggle
and conversation with friends in the hall, found Jesus.
Hallelujah. This is the man's own story : "For a long
time I have led a most dissipated and wicked life. Being
well connected, with wealthy friends, like the Prodigal,
I wandered into a far country; there I wasted my
substance in sin. In a short time I spent over two
hundred pounds. To-day I am a beggar, no one to take
me by the hand. Tired and weary in the past week, I
wandered about. It being a mission week, I wandered
into several churches, more for rest than to hear the
Word of God. Wherever I went the minister or preacher
seemed to be preaching to me. The first place I went
into he was speaking about the Prodigal Son. 'Ah,' said
I, 'that's me.' Strange to say, I went into another
church, and there I heard the same tale of the Prodigal
Son. The next night I went into another church, and
there I heard of the poor Prodigal. I asked myself the
question, what had I gained by my sin ?—a broken heart
and a wounded spirit. I had heard of a mission hall in
King Street, and I was rambling about to see if I could
get some place to sit down in, for I was tired. I happened

to be standing outside the hall at the end of the passage when a dear man came and invited me into the meeting. He gave me a little book to read, and as soon as ever I looked at it I found it was about the Prodigal Son. Tears rolled down my cheeks. I could not refrain from weeping bitterly as I thought of the past. I went into the hall and sat down, when I heard dear Mr. Holloway speak about the presence of the Master. The minister of the place came in. When prayers began I knelt down with the rest. When Mr. Hutton spoke to me about Jesus, saying, 'You are a poor Prodigal, my friend—read the 15th chapter of St. Luke, and may God bless you'—if any one had shot me I could not have been more struck. From first to last it was the Prodigal Son, which was a picture of myself. Only a few hours ago I had poison in my hands to take; but glory be to God for ever directing me into this mission hall." To have heard this young man pray in our meeting, during the mission, would have moved the hardest sinner. God opened a way for him, sent him a new suit of clothes, and a first-class situation in the city. He is now doing well.

Dear reader, are you a prodigal in sin? If so, there is mercy for you. Do not say you are too bad. The greater the sinner the more need of a Saviour. Christ turns none away—He wants to be gracious. None need perish—all may live, for Christ hath died. I laboured on, with mighty power from on high, not only inside but outside. Every night the place was crowded; and many, yea very many, were brought to Jesus. I have received several letters from persons who have been blessed, not only themselves but the whole family.

Many that were brought to a knowledge of the truth in Jesus brought their friends to hear the Gospel God moved among them and saved them. In several cases husband, wife, and two and three children, sisters and husbands, were saved. Praise the Lord. For it was and is marvellous in our eyes. "Salvation belongeth unto the

Lord ;" and if ever I felt the Holy Ghost at work it was at
this place. It had been arranged for a week of special
meetings in connection with different churches in London,
so that I went night after night with the following
brethren : Dr. Tomkins, J. T. Briscoe, T. Taylor, A. W.
Carmichael, and G. Hatton.

I returned to the King Street Hall and preached
another week, with much blessing. It was a pleasing sight
to see poor sinners, so worked upon by the Holy Spirit,
making their way into the vestries to give themselves to
Jesus. One man rose from his seat, one Saturday night,
called me to him and said, " I have heard a great deal
in my life, but never anything went to my heart before
like it has done to-night. By God's help, I'll start for
heaven." He left his name, and went home rejoicing in
the Lord. Another old man cried out, " Thank God, He
has saved me, though I am greyheaded—look at my bald
head. Christ has saved me." This happened before all the
people. One woman left the meeting to give her child
some food. She could not stay at home, being very
unhappy, and came back. When she again entered the
hall she found her husband on his knees crying for mercy.
Both husband and wife went home united to Christ, the
Living Vine. Praise the Lord. The time would fail to
tell of the wonderful dealings of God to poor perishing
sinners in this place. I left here amidst many greetings
from those who had found the Saviour, and also from all
the friends connected with the mission, who long to see
me return when they get into their new chapel at Wild
Street. May God give them souls there ; the Gospel is
much needed. I do pray that the Holy Spirit may light
up a pathway in our dear Brother Hatton's soul, that he
may be a burning and shining light to carry the Gospel to
the lost who are " dead in trespasses " and sin in this
Babylon of iniquity.

Having received a letter from Mr. John Stabb—who
for many years has devoted himself to the cause of God,

and with whom some of the readers of this book will be acquainted, I was sent by him, in the name of the Lord, to the Maryland Point Mission Hall, Stratford, where Mr. W. Andrews has been for the last three years in connection with this hall. Truly God led me there. After the first week's service, the following appeared in *The Christian* :—

"A GOOD WORK AT STRATFORD.—Assisted by the generous co-operation of Mr. John Stabb, whose work in connection with the schools and mission at Maryland Point, Stratford, is well known to many of our London readers, Henry Holloway has for more than a week been conducting a series of meetings in this locality. These meetings have been very numerously attended, and their spiritual results have been most encouraging. The spirit of prayer in connection with them, from the day on which the first was held until now, has, perhaps, been one of their chief characteristics.

"The subject of the first address was the Prodigal Son. The congregation was large, and had been gathered chiefly through the efforts of Mr. Andrews, the city missionary in this district; but the attention paid to the words spoken was all that could be desired. At the after-meeting many souls professed to have found Christ, the majority being men—some upwards of sixty years of age. Amongst them was one whose case presented singular features of interest. At the first after-meeting Mr. Andrews observed a man evidently under deep emotion, and spoke a kind and hopeful word to him, and advised him without a moment's delay to trust his all to Jesus. His reply was 'Not to-night.' By-and-by he crept towards the door and went out. The following night he came again, evidently under conviction of sin. Upon his buying one of Mr. Holloway's autobiographies, the latter said to him, 'I do hope, my brother, this book will bring you to your knees in prayer.' He went home and read it, and kept reading and thinking until a little after midnight. Then he suddenly said to his wife, 'Let us pray!' He was sorry, he said, that he left the after-meeting; but that, if God would spare him, he would go again; and he was as good as his word. He came the next night with a Bible under his arm. He was asked whether he had decided for Christ. He did decide that night, and went home a rejoicing man. He went singing through the streets, 'There is a fountain filled with blood.' He has since taken great interest in inducing others to come to the meetings, that they may be benefited as he has been.

"The Monday night meeting was a crowded one, and it was a season of great spiritual conflict for many. In fact, one who was present described it as 'a heavy struggle between the power of the Holy Spirit and the power of the devil.' Mr. Holloway made a plain, direct appeal to the heart and conscience, and, until near eleven o'clock, he and others were engaged in earnestly talking with the anxious and sin-burdened. Many professed to have found peace. It should be added that amongst these are men whose conversion would have belonging to it a contrast as striking as between darkness and light, death and life.

"Every night throughout the week the place has been full; but on Friday night it was crammed to the door, and a very earnest spirit pervaded the meeting. About two hundred persons have remained to the after-meetings for special prayer and conversation. Some of those who have been led to the Saviour belong to the railway works, and have carried the good news with them into the scene of their daily labour. The result has been that others have been led to attend the meetings, and some have gone home praising the Lord. The instances of good received have been most remarkable, especially amongst the very poor. Mr. Andrews, on visiting a poor woman, found her in the deepest poverty; but although she had not a crust she had found Christ. On his way to see her, he was accosted by a man who had been attending the meetings. 'I am anxious about my soul. Pray for me!' His request was complied with. The next day the man came to a meeting, his doubts were cleared away, and he went home rejoicing in the Lord.

"It has been no unusual thing at some of the after-meetings to see persons weeping, and smitten almost to the ground, under a sense of sin. There has, however, been no excitement in such cases. The word has been brought to bear upon them in their anxious state. It has revealed to them clearly what they are in God's sight, but just as clearly it has revealed that Christ is the Saviour for them. On Sunday evening last, the attendance was large, and Mr. Holloway's address on 'Fear thou not' was well adapted to encourage those in whose hearts a good work had been begun. The meetings will be continued throughout this week."

The following appeared in the *Stratford Express :—*

"Sir,—Can you find a corner in your columns for a word or two about the praiseworthy enterprise in which Mr. H. Holloway is engaged for the benefit of the working classes in Stratford, especially those residing in the New Town? His work, week by week, appears to awaken a more lively interest amongst those whose spiritual profit he aims to promote; and he has, therefore, a claim upon the sympathy and co-operation of all who believe that the working-man has religious duties, as well as political rights and privileges, which ought never to be lost sight of. It is no secret that in former years Mr. Holloway was a convict. Having by the grace of God 'put on the new man,' it is now the earnest aim of his life to make known to others the Saviour who found him in his hour of bitter need. His plain 'words in season' to his working-class brethren, whose temptations he knows by bitter experience, have come home to the hearts of many, and have led to 'new-ness of life' on the part of some of the most abandoned. No one can attend the meetings, which he holds almost every night in the week, without feeling that a blessing is attending his efforts. These meetings are crowded, and religious impressions have been made which have proved salutary and abiding. To my own mind, it does not admit of a moment's question, that in the Evangelistic work which he has so well begun he should be vigorously and generously sustained. To the utmost of my ability I have been ready to co-operate with him; but is not this the kind of work in which many would feel pleasure in taking part? Many, for a lengthened period, have been most desirous of the Gospel message being delivered to the working classes in your New Town. By Mr. Holloway's efforts this is now being done, unostentatiously—and successfully.—I am, Sir, your obedient servant,

"JOHN STABB."

After another week of untiring labour for precious souls, the following appeared in *The Christian* :—

"THE GOOD WORK AT STRATFORD.—It is pleasant to be able to report satisfactorily on the good work which has been commenced in this town. Every night last week the meetings at Maryland Point were numerously attended, and on more than one occasion the room was crammed. The addresses of Mr. Holloway have been listened to with the deepest interest, and in the after-meetings numbers of anxious inquirers have been conversed with, and have found peace in Jesus. Very satisfactory it is to state that amongst those attending the meetings have been men from the Great Eastern Railway Works in the town, and the testimony of one with whom the writer conversed was that the impression produced on many minds has been most salutary. It is proposed that Mr. Holloway should continue holding services in this locality for some time to come, and prayer is earnestly solicited on his behalf, that the divine blessing may continue to attend his efforts. The number of men present at the various meetings has been a pleasant characteristic of them, as hitherto it has been most difficult to secure their attendance at any religious gathering. Those who have been co-operating with Mr. Holloway have been greatly encouraged, and they continue to hope and pray that what they have seen is but the beginning of good things to come."

Also this,

" GOOD WORK AT STRATFORD.—Join with us in praise, for we have already God's answer to united prayer for the youth of our land. Upwards of twenty young people of the various churches (some new converts) have come forward to form an Evangelistic band, to commence work for the Lord, in the open air. Some have given themselves to distribution of tracts and singing, others to prayer and holding forth the Word of Life to poor sinners. The work of saving souls continues : also an earnest spirit is manifested everywhere. Earnest prayer is also desired for a yet greater blessing upon Brother H. Holloway's labours in this place, as some of the worst of persons have been and are being brought from darkness to light by the Word.—Yours faithfully, " JOHN STABB."

" New Bridge Street, Blackfriars."

" GOOD WORK AT STRATFORD.—Sir,—Could you allow me space in your columns to say a word about the labours of Mr. H. Holloway, of Manchester, among the working classes. He has given addresses every night, in Francis Street Mission School, for nearly a month, with great success. God has owned them, and they have been a great blessing to many families and young people, and the working classes will not hear of his leaving us. The aspect of many homes has been changed from sorrow and wretchedness to happiness and peace. On Friday, March 20th, the people were regaled with a bountiful tea, given by some gentlemen of the parish, after which a public meeting was held, presided over by Professor Jones, of Buxton College, and addresses given by Messers. Stabb, Lake, Andrews, and H. Holloway. Many were blessed indeed on that day, in such a manner as they never will forget, by the soul-stirring appeals that were made."

The work went on : for five weeks I preached the Gospel nearly every night, with much blessing. It was a very pleasing feature to see nightly upwards of fifty faces of dear working men and women at the meetings, whose faces carried the mark of their blessed Master, Jesus. Some of them had lived to the age of sixty years without God, and were only now brought to a knowledge of the truth that is in Jesus. I prayed that God might keep them from the evil that is in the world, and that they having put their hand to the plough might never look back. God grant that when temptation is nigh, the angels of the Lord may hover round and about them on every side, for Jesus Christ's sake. Amen.

Many will well remember the great Revival that took place throughout England, Ireland, and Scotland. It pleased God to bring about a glorious season of joy to many through the earnest and zealous labour of our dear brethren, Messrs. Moody and Sankey. At the time they came to Manchester I was conducting a mission in Manchester, laying myself out for usefulness in whatever way I could for the Lord, who had done so much for me. Night after night, when at liberty, I made my way to the Free Trade Hall, or the Oxford Hall, to do what I could in the after meetings conducted by Mr. Moody. It was at one of these meetings that I was introduced to a Mr. Henry Lakin, who once was a publican ; but God reached his heart, then down went the sign-board, " licensed to be drunk on the premises," and up went a sign with Gospel texts upon it—" God so loved the world," &c. John iii., 16. I gave him one of my books, " A Voice from the Convict Cell." Some days after this I received a letter from Satpin Hill, near Burton-upon-Trent, from Mr. Lakin. He had put my book into the hands of Mr. Guest, vicar of Christ Church, Burton. They invited me to Burton to hold services. I went, and my first meeting was in the St. George's Hall, and every week night in a mission church at the Waterside. Every night the place was full, many asking the question, " What must I do to be saved?" (Acts xvi., 30.) I could only stay eight days, having an engagement to fulfil at Derby. But, short as the stay was, I trust many were saved. I paid them a visit afterwards, in the church schools, and the meetings were crowded every night, God giving many blessings through the word preached. From here I went to Derby, and for over eight months, in the Gospel Hall in that town, in season and out of season, I held forth the glorious Gospel of the grace of God for nineteen weeks, night after night, with great blessing. Eternity will reveal all. Many of the dear friends whom God had blessed contributed voluntarily, and made me a present of a beautiful silver watch, with the following inscription inside: " Presented to Henry Holloway by his friends at the Derby Theatre Gospel Hall, Sept. 27th, 1875. On my departure to Liverpool Mr. G. Wilkins, superintendent of the mission, put a letter into my hand bearing the following : " Dear Bro. Holloway, this committee praise God unanimously for the great work God hath wrought through the preaching of the Gospel by you here ; and as you are about to go to Liverpool, we trust a similar blessing will attend your labours. Should the Lord lay it upon your heart to return to Derby you will write to us, and we will consider the praticability of your resuming your labours with us.—Yours truly, George Wilkins." I went to Liverpool for one month, and had just been there ten days when I received a telegram from Manchester informing me of my mother's illness. She had been suffering for some time from bronchitis, and she wished to see me before she went home. I had to give up preaching, took the midnight train to Manchester, and sat by her till she fell asleep in Jesus. The following is an account of her last words :—

As soon as I entered the house I saw her looking very pale ; a short hacking cough was troubling her. She looked at me and said, " Harry, my lad ; I am glad you have come, but sorry I had to send for you while you were doing the Lord's work, but I feel weak and near my journey's end here, and I longed to see you before I go home to heaven." Here she raised her eyes, and, looking up, said :—

I shall soon be at home over there,
For the end of my journey I see.

The chariots and the horsemen are coming ;
On earth I am a stranger
While passing through this vale of woe.
But, oh, how often danger attends the path wherein I go,
But Jesus Christ is with me I know.
He takes me by the hand ;
He says I'll never, never leave thee
Until thou art safe in the Promised Land.

I then asked her had she any doubt as to her acceptance by God. "Doubt, Harry, my lad ! Why do you ask me this ?" "Well, Mother," I said, "I have a reason." She replied, "For many years I have been trusting in the finished work of Jesus. I know and believe that my Saviour shed His precious blood, and the blood is the life, and cleanses from all sin. God's Word says it, and I believe it. So this clears all doubt away. This time to-morrow my soul will be at rest with God." Here a fit of coughing seized her. She began to vomit blood. "Mother," I said, "you are coughing up blood." Oh Jesus, come quickly." She said, "Blood did you say, Harry ? I am resting on the blood. Oh Harry, when I am gone tell poor sinners about the blood. Do go on trying to bring poor men and women to believe the truth of God's Word. And oh, my son, do keep out of the public-house, and live to glorify God. You will promise me you will never darken the door of a public-house, will you not, Harry ?" I said, "I will mother." "Live for God, work for Him, and you will get your reward, and meet me in heaven." While she was talking to me I sat by the bedside, now and then giving her a little beef tea ; this is all she could take. As the night came on she appeared to be nearing heaven, and was a deal worse. She asked me to send for the doctor again. He had been

F

once before. I fetched him, though late at night. When he came and looked at her he shook his head, called me on one side, and said give her all the comfort you can while she is here; she will not last more than three days at the longest. When I returned into the room mother looked at me. There was an heavenly smile upon her countenance. "Harry," said she, "what has the doctor been saying to you, my lad?" "Well, mother," I said, "he says you must have all the comfort you can here, for you will not live three days. "Three days," she said. "Ah, he is wrong, quite wrong. I shall be in glory with Jesus in the morning." (God had surely communicated to her by His Spirit that such should be the case, for as soon as the morning set in she was loosed from her suffering, and fell asleep in Him who died to redeem her.) A little after midnight she asked me to raise her head. I did so. I then gave her a little beef tea. After she had taken it she said, "That is the last I shall take down here. I shall sup with Christ in the heavenly kingdom in a short time. Try and get asleep Harry, my lad, will you; you must be tired." I laid on the sofa for a few minutes, when my mother said, "Harry, Harry! Look! They have arrived; now you will have to let me go. My Master has come with the angels; let me go." I put my arm round her neck, and said, "Mother, when you are gone I shall miss you; but my loss will be your gain." "Yes, Harry; 'absent from the body, present with the Lord.' 'I know that my Redeemer liveth,' and now that I am going to see the King in His beauty, and to behold the face of Jesus, let me once more urge you, Harry, to seek the lost by doing all you can to bring sinners to the truth, as it is in Jesus. Ah, Jesus! Is not that a sweet name! Jesus, Jesus, Jesus! Let me go to Jesus, Harry; let me go!" I held her hand in mine. My left hand was under her head, my right clasped hers. I did not want to part with her, bu I knew she was going to heaven. She turned her eyes on me and said, "The hour of my departure is near. They have already come. Dd you see, my lad?" "No, mother, I see nothing," I said. "Well, Harry, now I am going. Thank God the desire of my heart has been fulfilled—I have lived to see you converted. Tell Robert and James (these were my two brothers) that I died resting on the finished work of Jesus. He died for me, He gave His life for me, and now I go the way of all the earth. They are waiting for me! Jesus has come! Listen, Harry! Hark! Here she made a pause. Something was rattling in her throat, her eyes were cast up to the ceiling; in the room all was silent as death. The glory of God seemed to fill the place. She coughed. A small quantity of blood came out of her mouth, which I wiped away. She then closed her eyes, but in a moment she opened them again and looked at me, and said, "Harry, kiss me; the moment has come. I am ready, Jesus! Farewell, my lad. Tell all your friends my last moments were the BEST. Good bye! Not a DOUBT, Harry! The blood has been SHED, and I am going to be with JESUS! JESUS! JESUS!"

These were the last words she uttered, and then fell asleep. Reader, do you say, after reading these pages, "Let me die the death of the righteous, and let my last end be like hers." Well, it may be so; but are you living the life of the righteous? If you were to die this day would you go to heaven? Do you say No? Then where would you go? Oh, reader, I entreat thee, in the name of Jesus Christ, the Saviour of sinners, to stop and think before you further go. This night thy soul may be required of thee, and whose fault will it be if you do not get to heaven? Ponder these words, and resolve at once to give God what belongs to Him—that is your soul.

After my mother had gone home to heaven I went back to Derby to have one special meeting, to give an address upon my mother's last words, my mother having had the pleasure of visiting Derby while I was preaching there, and knowing—or rather becoming acquainted—with a great many friends. I gave an account of her last words, the hall being quite full, though the weather was very unfavourable ; and I have great reason to believe God blessed and owned His Word that night preached unto the people. I do trust that, as I have lost my best earthly friend (my mother) I may always remember I have a heavenly one, who has promised never to leave me nor forsake me. He will be our guide even unto death. May you, dear reader, trust Him—live to serve Him—and then death will not terrify you ; but you can say, "O Death, where is thy sting? O Grave, where is thy victory? The sting of death is sin, and the strength of sin is the law." But thanks be to God, which giveth us the victory through our Lord Jesus Christ." After mother's death I went to Scotland, as you will see by the following.

GLASGOW.—"God has chosen the foolish things of the world to confound the wise, and the weak things of the world to confound the things which are mighty ; and base things of the world, and things which are despised, hath God chosen—yea, and things which are not, to bring to nought things that are."

This portion of the Word has been exemplified during the past fortnight in this city through the instrumentality of Henry Holloway, of Manchester, who for some years back has been preaching the Gospel among the lost. Any one who saw him, some fourteen years ago, stand before the judge and jury in the court-house of Manchester, and heard the sentence of seven years' penal servitude passed upon him, would have been inclined to say it was impossible that that man could ever become a successful preacher of the Gospel of Christ ; but oh ! the riches of the grace of God in finding this lost one, and bringing him to the feet of Jesus. He is indeed a trophy of grace. The Lord had a mission for him, and has now made him a chosen vessel to carry His name among the outcasts of society. It has always been a difficulty with ministers and Christian workers how to reach this special class of people ; but by getting such men as Henry Holloway or Joshua Poole, who understand all their ways, the difficulty seems to vanish, and instead of finding it difficult to get the people to hear, it has been difficult to provide accommodation for all who came. Mr. Holloway's addresses are plain and practical, as well as interesting and attractive; his large and varied experience, backed up with a knowledge of the Word of God, makes him a successful preacher, and one whom God can use. He came to Glasgow under the auspices of the Orphan Home Mission (Mr. Quarrier, Glasgow), and the first meeting was the eight o'clock morning breakfast in the Drill Hall, when over 2,000 men and women had assembled to partake of the substantial breakfast provided for them every Sunday by the United Evangelistic Committee; the attention of the people was very marked, and it was most interesting to see many of the roughest characters in the hall come up to shake hands with the preacher, and to say they would come to talk with him privately at night. At eleven o'clock he again spoke in the same hall, and in the evening in the Orphan Home Hall. Long before the hour of commencing this building was packed to the doors as well as the side rooms, and hundreds were sent away for want of room. The Word was with power, and many waited to the after-meeting and were made happy in the Saviour's love. The meetings were conducted in the same building every night during the week, and resulted in much blessing. On the following Sunday the meeting was held in the Albion Hall, which is seated for 2,000 persons. This place was also crowded to the doors, and numbers could not gain admission.

Mr. Holloway has been visiting some of the low lodging-houses where hundreds of men come to sleep at night. At one of those places on Sunday afternoon he had nearly 200 men in the room; while he talked to them, understanding as he did all about them, they gave the greatest attention to what he had to say, and it has been pleasing to see them at the meetings every night since. Prayer was asked in *Word and Work* some weeks ago for blessing on these meetings, and now will the Lord's children join in praising our loving Father for his faithfulness in so abundantly answering.

As the meetings are to be continued for some time yet, earnest prayer is asked that the blessing already seen may be but the droppings of a mighty shower.—*Word and Work*, Nov. 2, 1876. RICHARD H. HUNTER.

GLASGOW.—With the departure of the Amercican evangelists we seem to have got over the heat of "revivalism," at least in the direction more particularly mapped out for Transatlantic evangelization. Looking back to that period, it seems strange that the soul-stiring blast of the American gospel-trumpet never shook the dry bones hidden away out of sight of respectacle society in the far back-grounds of dusky wynds and vennels. That promising field, however, has been taken up by a stranger nearer the doors, who in his own way, has been as great a success as the American revivalists in point of attraction. The individual announces himself as "A Voice from the Convict Cell." His name is Henry Holloway, and at first sight it may seem against him that he is a returned convict. That ugly fact, however, appeals powerfully to the sympathies of the class amongst whom he labours. In introducing Mr. Holloway it is not necessary to go over his previous life in detail. He is of humble parentage; a native of Birmingham, and having the misfortune to lose his father in childhood, came under the dominion of a cruel stepfather, who drove him from home, and cast him on the streets. Henry became associated with evil companions, who quickly led him astray and taught him to steal. After filling up his measure of folly, he ended by becoming a felon, and was sentenced to seven years' penal servitude. His mother's prayers, however seem to have followed him to his lonely cell, and through the instrumentality of a prison philanthropist he was converted. In a little book written by himself, from which he takes his *nom de plume,* an interesting account of his life before and after his reclamation is given. Meanwhile let us take a glance at him at mission work, under the auspices of the Orphan Home Mission. Some idea of Mr. Holloway's success in attracting crowds may be gathered from the fact that in all the various halls in Glasgow in which he has been announced to appear, the audience has been in excess of the accommodation provided, and the discomfort of crushing was cheerfully borne to obtain a hearing. It would appear also as if something more than novelty draws the multitude after him, for night after night the self-same shawls and faces make up the eager throng around the doors. Those who at first came out of mere curiosity to see a converted thief, continue to come as if they could'nt help it. But, step inside, it is the last night of " A Voice from the Convict Cell," in the Victoria Theatre, Anderston. Eight o'clock has just struck, and the police are passing in the audience at the Victoria, long before the stage is occupied. Boxes, pit, and gallery are filled to overflowing, Let us take a look at the motley groups, packed up promiscuously in the free seats all over the house. There is no dress circle, but most of the ladies are without bonnets, and some have not particularly clean faces. Amongst the elderly portion, worsted caps ; girls in bare heads, but tidy-looking, come next ; then a sprinkling of jaunty hats, with a feather to distinguish the social position of the wearer ; then a row of matrons, with their features half-buried in colourless shawls, and their arms filled with sleepy bairns; respectable women, well dressed, and comely; disreputable females in dirt and rags, cowering behind them ; round-eyed children and aged grandames, all mixed up together in bewildering confusion. The men are a more curious study. You can tell almost their occupations from their countenances. The complement is made up far back in the shade by a group of smartly attired girls, whose gaudy finery and painted faces declare their calling. When the services commence all is attention;

but it is easily to perceive all the interest lies in Henry Holloway. The preliminary hymns, however, are heartily sung, "A Voice from the Convict Cell" rises, and there is a sudden wakening up. Henry Holloway does not come up to the familiar type of prison-bird; he has a pleasant countenance, a clear, ringing voice, and a happy sense of the humorous, and is, in a word, altogether the reverse from what one would expect to see from the character he has been. He makes no attempt at display, and does not take time to pick up his "H's" and "I's;" but he manages to make a wonderful impression upon his hearers by his simple earnestness, and his happy knack of arresting attention on the ground of a common experience. He knows to a "t" the people he is dealing with, and never for a moment loses his identity with them. He might be called slightly egotistical in his personal illustrations with a different audience, but it is only by speaking the language they best understand and identifying himself with their "order," that he could produce any lasting impression on his hearers. The Bible is a sealed book to them, but they can catch some meaning by a familar illustration, and this is the way Henry Holloway carries his hearers along with him—" There's the lighthouse lamp at Gibralter; I gave it three coats of paint, and then gilded its top until it shone again." Then he describes its bright and shining light, and the lonely prisoners looking up at it; and as the picture comes home to some present that he knows, he draws the Biblical comparison with telling effect. There can be no doubt of the impression he makes and of the good that might result from his preaching. It is four years since he commenced mission work, and the success which has attended his labours is the best praise that can be bestowed upon him. He is not a paid agent although a poor man, but his wants have always been supplied.—*North British Daily Mail.*

DALKEITH, N.B.—Prayer was lately asked for a series of evangelistic meetings to be conducted by Mr, Henry

Holloway, of Manchester, in this town. We rejoice to give thanks and praise to our heavenly Father for the rich blessings we have received. Special efforts have been put forth several times to awaken the working classes and bring them under the sound of the Gospel, but have in most cases proved a failure. However, when our friend and brother Henry Holloway was announced to hold meetings a deep interest was awakened, and the first meeting was filled to overflowing; numbers could not gain admittance, and many were standing in the lobbies and on the stairs willing to *hear*, although they could not *see* the speaker. All through the fortnight that he has been preaching the meetings have been filled, many attending most regularly who have for years refused to enter any place to hear the Gospel. The result of these meetings will be known when the Lord comes to make up his jewels. Several ministers of the town have taken part in the services. We exceedingly regret our brother's departure so soon, but he having to return to Glasgow, thence to Richmond, cannot prolong his stay here at present.—*The Christian, Jan. 11th, 1877.*

W. TOD.

And now, reader, what do you think of all that is in this book? Referring to the goodness of God to poor sinners, and such as I have been, do you say you have not been as bad as me, or you would repent and turn to God? You need not be as bad as me to be lost. Let me warn you as one that loves you, to give yourself to Christ at once. Beware of the public-house : it is the fool's college. If you are a working man, and have to work hard for your living, don't let the public-houses work you into them. Oh, let me entreat of you to make no more delay : go at once to Jesus with that faith and assurance which will bring the blessing to your soul. Don't forget, however bad you have been, that none need perish : all may live, for Christ hath died. Remember, the writer has been as near hell as anyone out of it; and, as one who wishes to be all things to all men, that he may win some, he holds himself up as a monument of God's saving mercy and redeeming love; and

> I never shall forget the day
> When Jesus washed my sins away.

Happy is my life, and all other men who have Christ in their hearts—the evidence of eternal glory; in order to attain which, pray fervently, believe firmly, wait patiently, work diligently, live holy, die daily, watch your heart, guard your senses, redeem your time, love Christ, and long for glory. Look to Jesus at all times—always, under every circumstance: look to Jesus when tempted, when afflicted, when troubled, when sick, when in health, when oppressed, when rich, when poor, when forsaken, when dying. If you do this, you will never repent this little book being placed in your hand. Do I hear you say, "I hope to go to heaven?" This is a common expression. On what foundation does your hope rest? What reason have you to expect you will go to heaven when you die? Heaven is a prepared place for a prepared people. Though it is the abode of perfect and everlasting happiness, yet none reach that pure and blissful place but those "who have washed their robes, and made them white in the blood of the Lamb." By nature and practice we are all sinful and defiled; therefore, we must be pardoned and cleansed from our sins before we can enter into the presence of the Holy Lord God Almighty. Those whose hearts are unchanged would not be happy, even were it possible for them to enter heaven; for all the inhabitants and all the employments of that place are holy and spiritual. Unless your hearts are changed by the grace of Christ here, they cannot be fitted for the presence of Christ hereafter. "Except a man be born again, he cannot see the kingdom of God." (John iii., 3.) Therefore, seek now the pardon of your sins through the blood of Christ, for the time is at hand when He who is now proclaimed as the Saviour of sinners shall pass His sentence. "He that is unjust, let him be unjust still; and he which is filthy let him be filthy still; and he that is righteous, let him be righteous still; and he that is holy, let him be holy still. And, behold, I come quickly; and my reward is with me, to give every man according as his work shall be." (Rev. xxii., 11, 12.)

Do you ask, "What must I do to be saved?" The answer I give to this question—let the word of God speak to you—"Believe on the Lord Jesus Christ, and thou shalt be saved. (Acts xvi., 30, 31.) But how am I to believe? "If thou shalt confess with thy mouth the Lord Jesus, and shalt believe in thine heart that God hath raised Him from the dead, thou shalt be saved. For with the heart man believeth unto righteousness; and with the mouth confession is made unto salvation. For the Scripture saith, Whosoever believeth on Him (Jesus) shall not be ashamed. For whosoever shall call upon the name of the Lord shall be saved." (Romans x., 9–13.) For "It is faithful saying, and worthy of all acceptation, that Christ Jesus came into the world to save sinners." "For God so loved the world that He gave His only begotten Son, that whosoever believeth in Him should not perish, but have everlasting life." Take warning, reader. "He that believeth on Him is not condemned; but he that believeth not is condemned ALREADY." Dear friend, whoever you are, rich or poor, learned or unlearned, bond or free, if you are unsaved, what an awful position you are in! "Condemned already"—waiting for judgment!

Let me take you before an earthly judge, one that has power to send a man to prison if he breaks the law. There stands the prisoner at the bar; and after a lengthened trial, the jury are asked the question, "Do you find the prisoner guilty or not guilty?" "Guilty!" After the prisoner is found guilty, the judge defers passing sentence then, and puts it off till another time. Reader, if you are unsaved, God holds you guilty of the murder of His Son, Jesus Christ: you are under condemnation; and the only reason I can give you that God has not cut you off in the midst of your sins, and consigned you to endless misery, is because God loves you : "He sent not His Son into the world to condemn the world, but that the world through Him might be saved." God wants you to be saved. He waits to be gracious. It is not His will that any should perish, but that all should be saved. If you are lost it will be your own fault. Read the sixteenth chapter of St. Luke, from the nineteenth verse to the end. May God help you to escape for your life ! Where to ? To Christ, the sinner's friend.

> None but Jesus, none but Jesus,
> Can do helpless sinners good.

You may say all this is very good, but you don't know what a sinner I am. This may be true ; I don't know ; but I can tell you this, my brother or sister, if you know you are sinners, and you see the need of a friend to help you, go to Jesus ; for "the Son of man is come to seek and to save that which was lost." Do you say you are not lost ? If you are unsaved you are lost, and you cannot be found without you are lost : so, if you will not confess you are lost, ruined, and undone, without Christ, you will be lost for ever and for ever. There is no way of escape but through Christ. If you meet God at all to receive pardon for your sins, you will have to meet Him in Christ. The Bible says so. Let this be true, and every man a liar. Remember, reader, heaven and earth may pass away, but God's Word shall never pass away. Then let me beseech you, my friend, before you read another line, to ask God to save you ; if it is only a short prayer like that of the dying thief upon the cross, " Lord, remember me."—Luke xxiii., 42. God commands that faith that will not take a denial. Read the fifteenth chapter of the Gospel according to St. Matthew, from the 22nd to the 29th verse. Let your prayer be like that poor woman's, " Lord, help me ;" or like Peter's when he was sinking upon the sea, " Lord, save me." (Matt. xiv., 30.)

Do you say, after all, "This is very good, but you do not know what I have done in my life. I have beat my wife, starved my children, wronged my master, and committed a thousand other crimes which nobody knows about." Yes, my friend, God knows it all; and God alone, through Christ, can pardon thee, for "whosoever believeth shall be saved." Suppose you, reader, were going along some fields, and you saw a signboard with the following inscription upon it: "Whosoever is found trespassing on this ground will be prosecuted," would you not understand at once that the word "whosoever" included you? So, my brother or sister, when God's word says, "Whosoever will may come," it includes you. Believe God's word, and you are safe; reject it, and you are lost. Remember, friend, however long you keep back, if you are to be saved you will have to come to the same way at last. There is no mediator between God and man, but the man Christ Jesus.

Can you say, if God should stop your breath this moment, you are prepared for heaven? If a friend were asking you this to your face, instead of me, through this book, you might say, Yes, and he would know no difference, because he could only see your face; but, remember, there is one that can penetrate the inmost recesses of your heart. God knows all about you. You may deceive man —God you cannot. "Be ye also ready, for in such an hour as ye think not the Son of man cometh." While I am writing these pages I am thinking of what I once was, and what I am now. "Bless the Lord, O my soul, and all that is within me bless his holy name."

Jesus sought me when a stranger,
Wandering from the fold of God;
And to rescue me from danger,
Upon the cross He shed His blood.

I was like a poor lost sheep going astray; yes, I had quite gone out of the way; but Jesus found me in the mire and clay, and set me on the rock of ages. "My beloved is mine, and I am his." I am sheltered beneath the cross.

I have a friend which to me is "the fairest among ten thousand, and the altogether lovely." He is "the rose of Sharon and the lily of the valleys." He is "the way, the truth, and the life;" "the bright and the morning star;" "the brightness of the Father's glory, and the express image of his person." He is "the first and the last," Thank God, He is my Saviour, for He has saved me.

And now, dear reader, I must close. I may just say I am at present labouring among the working classes of Glasgow, having been invited by Mr. W. Quarrier and Mr. R. Hunter, in connection with the City Orphan Home Mission. For some weeks God has been doing great things in our midst. Some of the very vilest of men and women have been drawn together to hear the old, old story of Jesus and His love. Many times I have seen the Victoria Music Hall densely packed with nearly three thousand souls to hear the glorious Gospel of the blessed God; and not a few, I trust, have, through the Word preached unto them, decided to go and sin no more. I trust my life may be long spared to publish the good news of the Gospel to poor perishing sinners, so that at last I may come to His eternal joy, through Jesus Christ my Lord, to meet my mother, who is "not dead but gone before." Reader, art thou on thy way to heaven or going the downward course to hell? I beseech thee, consider now, ere you take another step. Stop, and think—after death the judgment. Remember now, this moment, there is pardon, peace, and rest through the blood of Jesus alone. No other. He is the way, the truth, the life. Death through sin; life through Christ. Believe on the Lord Jesus Christ and thou shalt be saved. But believe now. "Now is the accepted time; behold, now is the day of salvation." Reader, shall I meet you in heaven?

Dear reader, when I look at the teeming masses that are living in sin, I am reminded of a case that came under my notice a short time ago. A friend of mine came to me and said, "Mr. Holloway, I have been in such great trouble to-day." "What's the matter?" said I. "Why," said he, "one of my little lads went astray from home, and he has been lost about six hours. I and my dear wife sought him high and low, almost broken-hearted; and, at last, where do you think we found him? In the gutter, in one of the back streets, some distance from our house; and there he was sitting round a heap of dirt which he had collected together by means of a piece of wood which he had in his hand."

Reader, he was playing with this dirt, and seemed quite at home, notwithstanding the time he had been away; and it was very evident he had had nothing to eat all the time he had been away from home.

When the father saw him he ran up to him with joy, and clasped him to his bosom; but after all this the child cried to stay and play with his dirt, preferring rather to sit in the gutter than go with his father to a happy, comfortable home. Is not this the character of every poor unsaved sinner who is wandering from God his Father? Though Jesus Christ seeks you, and entreats you to come home, you choose rather to hold to your sin, like a miser would to his gold, before you will come and be saved, and be made a partaker of a heavenly mansion which God your Father has prepared for you. Oh, dear reader, let me ask you not to take another step in sin. Lay down the weapons of your rebellion, and fight against God no longer. He waits to be gracious. Is he not a friend? Yes, He has been a friend to you ever since you were born. He has been about your bed and about your path, about your going out and coming in; in short, he hath died for you. Christ died for you! However vile you are there is redemption through the precious blood of Christ. The precious blood! When I was a poor prisoner I remember seeing a prisoner brought out to be flogged for breaking the laws of the prison. The charge was read, the triangle was brought out, and the prisoner was strapped up by his arms and legs. A number of prisoners brought the scene as a kind of caution to them. The officer that flogged the man was told to do his duty. Each lash (he was to have fifty) told a tale upon the prisoner's back. When he had received about twenty-five, a poor prisoner that was looking on at the scene, filled with love and sympathy for his fellow-prisoner, rushed from the wall towards the triangle, and cried, "For God's sake, give the man no more; let me take the rest of his lashes." Dear reader, was not this love on behalf of this poor prisoner? When I witnessed the scene I thought of God's wondrous love to man. You and I have broken God's laws. The penalty due to us is death, for "the wages of sin is death." (Romans vi., 23.) God has satisfied the law in giving His only Son to die for sinners; and when justice would have cut you and I down, Jesus came forth and gave "His back to the smiters, and His cheeks to them that plucked off the hair." He died for thee. Reader, what hast thou done for Him? Once more I entreat you, as an ambassador for Christ—"I beseech you, in Christ's stead, be ye reconciled to God." May you and I have the happy pleasure of meeting in Heaven! Amen.

JOHN HEYWOOD, Excelsior Printing and Stationery Works, Hulme Hall Road, Manchester.

Second Edition.—Fortieth Thousand.

—

# AN ECHO FROM PRISON;

OR,

# MY MOTHER AND I.

=====

CAN BE HAD FROM THE PUBLISHER,

# PRICE ONE PENNY.

*12 copies post-free; or 6s. per 100 for circulation.*

—

**JOHN HEYWOOD, 141 & 143, DEANSGATE, MANCHESTER.**

OR FROM

HENRY HOLLOWAY,

CITY ORPHAN HOME,

JAMES MORRISON STREET,

GLASGOW.

# HYMN.

What a Captain I have got!
Is not this a happy lot?
Therefore will I take the sword,
Fight for Jesus Christ my Lord.

  *Chorus.* — His soldier sure shall be
   Happy in eternity.

I by faith enlisted am
In the service of the Lamb;
Pleasant pay I now receive,
... each shall give.

  *Chorus.* — His soldier, &c.

... He sits on ... ,
... poor sinners still.
Will you see ... King?
Come, enlist, and you will sing.

  *Chorus.* — His soldier, &c.

Oh, come, my friends, and go with me,
... the celestial see;
Should you get there before I ...,
Look out for me, I am coming ...

  *Chorus.* — His soldier, &c.

Parents and children ... soldiers.
Husbands, and wives, and friends so dear.
Then, come, my friends, and go with me,
I'm going the Saviour's face to see.

  *Chorus.* — His soldier, &c.

www.ingramcontent.com/pod-product-compliance
Lightning Source LLC
LaVergne TN
LVHW061220060426
835508LV00014B/1373

*9781535815802*